*Praise for* The Moment of Lift

'Melinda Gates has spent many years working with women around the world. This book charts her own evolution as a feminist and celebrates the stories of others who inspired her on her journey. It is an urgent manifesto for an equal society where women are valued and recognized in all spheres of life. Most of all, it is a call for unity, inclusion and connection. We need this message more than ever.'   Malala Yousafzai

'Melinda tells the stories of the inspiring people she's met through her work all over the world, digs into the data, and powerfully illustrates issues that need our attention – from child marriage to gender inequity in the workplace.'   President Barack Obama

'Full of personal moving anecdotes from women she's met all over the world, along with cold, hard facts showing that economies will thrive if we're all equal.'   *Scotsman*

'An illuminating and often moving scrutiny of the ways in which the lot of women can be improved.'   *Observer*

'A book – part memoir, part manifesto – about how empowering women everywhere, from sub-Saharan Africa to Appalachian America, is the key to a better world.'   *Sunday Times* magazine

'An inspirational look at the need to empower women to make change in the world.'   *Washington Post*

'For the past two decades, Melinda Gates has been a force, and an increasingly forceful voice, in global health. Yet *The Moment of Lift* is a book about gender equity and its golden thread is empathy. This book lifts up the voices of women and girls whose experiences have been entirely unlike Melinda's own. They've taught her a great deal, and in this beautifully crafted and artful memoir, Melinda Gates invites the reader to learn from them too.'

Paul Farmer, MD, Kolokotrones University Professor,
alth

9030   D0231579

'*The Moment of Lift* reveals painful truths about women living in the most vulnerable areas of the world. Melinda Gates uplifts and inspires by weaving a narrative of fortitude and hope. She pushes us to challenge the status quo and never settle.'
Mellody Hobson

'I think this is one of the best books I've ever read.' Warren Buffett

'A moral appeal, imploring each of us who reads it to look around – at our own families, our own workplaces, our own place in a gigantic, but highly connected, world – and get to work making it more equal.'
*Chicago Tribune*

'Melinda Gates's book is a lesson in listening. A powerful, poignant, and ultimately humble call to arms.'
Tara Westover, author of *Educated*

'*The Moment of Lift* is an urgent call to courage. It changed how I think about myself, my family, my work, and what's possible in the world. Melinda weaves together vulnerable, brave storytelling and compelling data to make this one of those rare books that you carry in your heart and mind long after the last page.'
Brené Brown, Ph.D., author of *New York Times* #1
bestseller *Dare to Lead*

'This book is a beautiful and concise mission statement on what we need to do to move society forward- continue to empower women. At every level and in all places women are truly the bedrock supporting their communities.'
Trevor Noah

# THE MOMENT OF LIFT

## EMPOWERING WOMEN CHANGES THE WORLD

## MELINDA GATES

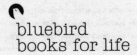

bluebird
books for life

First published 2019 by Flatiron Books
First published in the UK 2019 by Bluebird.

This edition first published 2020 by Bluebird,
an imprint of Pan Macmillan
The Smithson, 6 Briset Street, London EC1M 5NR
Associated companies throughout the world
www.panmacmillan.com

ISBN 978-1-5290-0551-6

Copyright © Melinda Gates 2019

The right of Melinda Gates to be identified as the
author of this work has been asserted by her in accordance
with the Copyright, Designs and Patents Act 1988.

All rights reserved. No part of this publication may be reproduced,
stored in a retrieval system, or transmitted, in any form, or by any means
(electronic, mechanical, photocopying, recording or otherwise)
without the prior written permission of the publisher.

Pan Macmillan does not have any control over, or any responsibility for,
any author or third-party websites referred to in or on this book.

135798642

A CIP catalogue record for this book is available from the British Library.

Printed and bound by CPI Group (UK) Ltd, Croydon, CR0 4YY

MIX
Paper from
responsible sources
FSC® C116313

This book is sold subject to the condition that it shall not, by way of
trade or otherwise, be lent, hired out, or otherwise circulated without
the publisher's prior consent in any form of binding or cover other than
that in which it is published and without a similar condition including
this condition being imposed on the subsequent purchaser.

Visit www.panmacmillan.com to read more about all our books
and to buy them. You will also find features, author interviews and
news of any author events, and you can sign up for e-newsletters
so that you're always first to hear about our new releases.

*For Jenn, Rory, and Phoebe*

| | |
|---|---|
| **LONDON BOROUGH OF WANDSWORTH** | |
| 9030 00007 1114 6 | |
| **Askews & Holts** | |
| 920 GATE | |
| | WW19017589 |

# Contents

*Our deepest fear is that we are powerful beyond measure.*

—MARIANNE WILLIAMSON

# Introduction

When I was little, space launches were a huge deal in my life. I grew up in Dallas, Texas, in a Catholic family with four kids, a stay-at-home mom, and an aerospace engineer dad who worked on the Apollo program.

On the day of a launch, we'd all pile into the car and drive to the home of one of my dad's friends—another Apollo engineer—and watch the drama together. I can still feel in my bones the suspense of those countdowns. *"Twenty seconds and counting, T minus fifteen seconds, guidance is internal, Twelve, Eleven, Ten, Nine, ignition sequence start, Six, Five, Four, Three, Two, One, Zero. All engines running. Liftoff! We have a liftoff!!!"*

Those moments always gave me a thrill—especially that moment of lift when the engines ignite, the earth shakes, and the rocket starts to rise. I recently came across the phrase "moment of lift" in a book by Mark Nepo, one of my favorite spiritual writers. He uses the words to capture a moment of grace. Something was "lifted like a scarf on the wind," he writes, and his grief went silent and he felt whole.

Mark's image of lift is filled with wonder. And wonder has two meanings for me. It can mean awe, and it can mean curiosity. I have loads of awe—but just as much curiosity. *I want to know how lift happens!*

At one time or another, we've all been sitting on a plane at the end of a long takeoff run, waiting anxiously for the moment of lift. When the kids were little and we were on a plane ready to take off, I'd say to them "wheels, wheels, wheels," and the moment the plane got off the ground I'd say *"Wings!!"* When the kids were a bit older, they would join me, and we all said it together for years. Once every so often, though, we'd say "wheels, wheels, wheels" more times than we expected, and I'd be thinking, *Why is it taking so long to get off the ground!?*

Why *does* it sometimes take so long? And why does it sometimes happen so fast? What takes us past the tipping point when the forces pushing us *up* overpower the forces pulling us *down* and we're lifted from the earth and begin to fly?

As I've traveled the world for twenty years doing the work of the foundation I cofounded with my husband, Bill, I've wondered:

How can we summon a moment of lift for human beings—and especially for women? Because when you lift up women, you lift up humanity.

And how can we create a moment of lift in human hearts so that we all *want* to lift up women? Because sometimes all that's needed to lift women up is to stop pulling them down.

In my travels, I've learned about hundreds of millions of women who want to decide for themselves whether and when to have children, but they can't. They have no access to contraceptives. And there are many other rights and privileges that women and girls are denied: The right to decide whether and when and whom to marry. The right to go to school. Earn an income. Work outside the home. *Walk* outside the home. Spend their own money. Shape their budget. Start a business. Get a loan. Own property. Divorce a husband. See a doctor. Run for office. Ride a bike. Drive a car. Go to college. Study computers. Find investors. All these rights are denied to women in some parts of the world. Sometimes these rights are denied under law, but even when they're allowed by law, they're still often denied by cultural bias against women.

My journey as a public advocate began with family planning. Later I started to speak up about other issues as well. But I quickly realized—because I was quickly *told*—that it wasn't enough to speak up for family planning, or even for each of the issues I've just named. I had to speak up for *women*. And I soon saw that if we are going to take our place as equals with men, it won't come from winning our rights one by one or step by step; we'll win our rights in waves as we become empowered.

These are lessons I've learned from the extraordinary people I want you to meet. Some will make your heart break. Others will make your heart *soar*. These heroes have built schools, saved lives, ended wars, empowered girls, and changed cultures. I think they'll inspire you. They've inspired me.

They've shown me the difference it makes when women are lifted up, and I want everyone to see it. They've shown me what people can do to make an impact, and I want everyone to know it. That is why I wrote this book: to share the stories of people who have given focus and urgency to my life. I want us to see the ways we can help each other flourish. The engines are igniting; the earth is shaking; we are rising. More than at any time in the past, we have the knowledge and energy and moral insight to crack the patterns of history. We need the help of every advocate now. Women and men. No one should be left out. Everyone should be brought in. Our call is to lift women up—and when we come together in this cause, *we are the lift*.

# CHAPTER ONE

# The Lift of a Great Idea

Let me start with some background. I attended Ursuline Academy, an all-girls Catholic high school in Dallas. In my senior year, I took a campus tour of Duke University and was awed by its computer science department. That decided it for me. I enrolled at Duke and graduated five years later with a bachelor's degree in computer science and a master's in business. Then I got a job offer from IBM, where I had worked for several summers, but I turned it down to take a job at a smallish software company called Microsoft. I spent nine years there in various positions, eventually becoming general manager of information products. Today I work in philanthropy, spending most of my time searching for ways to improve people's lives—and often worrying about the people I will fail if I don't get it right. I'm also the wife of Bill Gates. We got married on New Year's Day in 1994. We have three children.

That's the background. Now let me tell you a longer story—about my path to women's empowerment and how, as I've worked to empower others, others have empowered me.

In the fall of 1995, after Bill and I had been married nearly two years and were about to leave on a trip to China, I discovered I was pregnant. This China trip was a huge deal for us. Bill rarely took time off from Microsoft, and we were going with other couples as well. I didn't want to mess up the trip, so I considered not telling Bill I was pregnant until we came back. For a day and a half, I thought, *I'll just save the news.* Then I realized, *No, I've got to tell him because what if something goes wrong?* And, more basically, *I've got to tell him because it's his baby, too.*

When I sat Bill down for the baby talk one morning before work, he had two reactions. He was thrilled about the baby, and then he said, "You considered not telling me? Are you *kidding*?"

It hadn't taken me long to come up with my first bad parenting idea.

We went to China and had a fantastic trip. My pregnancy didn't affect things except for one moment when we were in an old museum in Western China and the curator opened an ancient mummy case; the smell sent me hurtling outside to avoid a rush of morning sickness—which I learned can come at any time of day! One of my girlfriends who saw me race out said to herself, "Melinda's pregnant."

On the way home from China, Bill and I split off from the group to get some time alone. During one of our talks, I shocked Bill when I said, "Look, I'm not going to keep working after I have this baby.

I'm not going back." He was stunned. "What do you *mean*, you're not going back?" And I said, "We're lucky enough not to need my income. So this is about how we want to raise a family. You're not going to downshift at work, and I don't see how I can put in the hours I need to do a great job at work and raise a family at the same time."

I'm offering you a candid account of this exchange with Bill to make an important point at the very start: When I first confronted the questions and challenges of being a working woman and a mother, I had some growing up to do. My personal model back then—and I don't think it was a very conscious model—was that when couples had children, men worked and women stayed home. Frankly, I think it's great if women want to stay home. But it should be a choice, not something we do because we think we have no choice. I don't regret my decision. I'd make it again. At the time, though, I just assumed that's what women do.

In fact, the first time I was asked if I was a feminist, I didn't know what to say because I didn't think of myself as a feminist. I'm not sure I knew then what a feminist was. That was when our daughter Jenn was a little less than a year old.

Twenty-two years later, I am an ardent feminist. To me, it's very simple. Being a feminist means believing that *every* woman should be able to use her voice and pursue her potential, and that women and men should all work together to take down the barriers and end the biases that still hold women back.

This isn't something I could have said with total conviction even ten years ago. It came to me only after many years of listening to women—often women in extreme hardship whose stories taught me what leads to inequity and how human beings flourish.

But those insights came to me later. Back in 1996, I was seeing everything through the lens of the gender roles I knew, and I told Bill, "I'm not going back."

This threw Bill for a loop. Me being at Microsoft was a huge part of our life together. Bill cofounded the company in 1975. I joined Microsoft in 1987, the only woman in the first class of MBAs. We met shortly afterward, at a company event. I was on a trip to New York for Microsoft, and my roommate (we doubled up back then to save money) told me to come to a dinner I hadn't known about. I showed up late, and all the tables were filled except one, which still had two empty chairs side by side. I sat in one of them. A few minutes later, Bill arrived and sat in the other.

We talked over dinner that evening, and I sensed that he was interested, but I didn't hear from him for a while. Then one Saturday afternoon we ran into each other in the company parking lot. He struck up a conversation and asked me out for two weeks from Friday. I laughed and said, "That's not spontaneous enough for me. Ask me out closer to the date," and I gave him my number. Two hours later, he called me at home and invited me out for that evening. "Is this spontaneous enough for you?" he asked.

We found we had a lot in common. We both love puzzles, and we both love to compete. So we had puzzle contests and played math games. I think he got intrigued when I beat him at a math game and won the first time we played Clue, the board game where you figure out who did the murder in what room with what weapon. He urged me to read *The Great Gatsby*, his favorite novel, and I already had, twice. Maybe that's when he knew he'd met his match. His *romantic* match, he would say. I knew I'd met my match when I saw his music collection—lots of Frank Sinatra and Dionne Warwick. When we got engaged, someone asked Bill, "How does Melinda make you feel?" and he answered, "Amazingly, she makes me feel like getting married."

Bill and I also shared a belief in the power and importance of software. We knew that writing software for personal computers would give individuals the computing power that institutions had, and democratizing computing would change the world. That's why we were so excited to be at Microsoft every day—going 120 miles an hour building software.

But our conversations about the baby made it clear that the days of our both working at Microsoft were ending—that even after the children were older, I would likely never go back there. I had wrestled with the idea before I was pregnant, talking with female friends and colleagues about it, but once Jenn was on the way, I had made up my mind. He didn't try to talk me out of it. He just kept asking, *"Really?!"*

As Jenn's birth approached, Bill started asking me, "Then what *are* you going to do?" I loved working so much that he couldn't imagine me giving up that part of my life. He was expecting me to get started on something new as soon as we had Jenn.

He wasn't wrong. I was soon searching for the right creative outlet, and the cause I was most passionate about when I left Microsoft was how you get girls and women involved in technology, because technology had done so much for me in high school, college, and beyond.

My teachers at Ursuline taught us the values of social justice and pushed us hard academically—but the school hadn't conquered the gender biases that were dominant then and prominent today. To give you a picture: There was a Catholic boys high school nearby, Jesuit Dallas, and we were considered brother-sister schools. We girls went to Jesuit to take calculus and physics, and the boys came to Ursuline to take typing.

Before I started my senior year, my math teacher, Mrs. Bauer, saw Apple II+ computers at a mathematics conference in Austin, returned to our school, and said, "We need to get these for the girls." The principal, Sister Rachel, asked, "What are we going to do with them if nobody knows how to use them?" Mrs. Bauer replied, "If you buy them, I'll learn how to teach them." So the school reached deep into the budget and made its first purchase of personal computers—*five* of them for the whole school of six hundred girls, and one thermal printer.

Mrs. Bauer spent her own time and money to drive to North Texas State University to study computer science at night so she could teach us in the morning. She ended up with a master's degree, and we had a blast. We created programs to solve math problems, converted numbers to different bases, and created primitive animated graphics. In one project, I programmed a square smiley face that moved around the screen in time to the Disney song "It's a Small World." It was rudimentary—computers couldn't do much with graphics back then—but I didn't know it was rudimentary. I was proud of it!

That's how I learned that I loved computers—through luck and the devotion of a great teacher who said, "We need to get these for the girls." She was the first advocate for women in tech I ever knew, and the coming years would show me how many more we need. College for me was coding with guys. My entering MBA class at Microsoft was all guys. When I went to Microsoft for my hiring interviews, all but one of the managers were guys. That didn't feel right to me.

I wanted women to get their share of these opportunities, and that became the focus of the first philanthropic work I got involved in—not long after Jenn was born. I thought the obvious way to get girls exposed to computers was to work with people in the local school district to help bring computers into public schools. I got deeply involved in several schools, getting them computerized. But the more I got into it, the more it became clear that it would be hugely expensive to try to expand access to computers by wiring every school in the country.

Bill believes passionately that technology should be for everyone, and at that time Microsoft was working on a small-scale project to give people access to the internet by donating computers to libraries. When Microsoft completed the project, they scheduled a meeting to present the results to Bill, and he said to me, "Hey, you should come learn about this. This is something we both might be interested in." After we heard the numbers, Bill and I said to each other, "Wow, maybe we should do this nationwide. What do you think?"

Our foundation was just a small endowment and an idea back then. We believed that all lives had equal value, but we saw that the world didn't act that way, that poverty and disease afflicted some places far more than others. We wanted to create a foundation to fight those inequities, but we didn't have anyone to lead it. I couldn't run it, because I wasn't going to go back to a full work schedule while I had little kids. At that time, though, Patty Stonesifer, the top woman executive at Microsoft and someone Bill and I both respected and admired, was leaving her job, and we had the temerity to approach her at her farewell party and ask her if she would run this project. She said yes and became the first foundation employee, working for free in a tiny office above a pizza parlor.

That's how we got started in philanthropy. I had the time to get involved when I was still at home with Jenn because we didn't have our son, Rory, until Jenn was 3 years old.

I realize in looking back that I faced a life-forming question in those early years: "Do you want to have a career or do you want to be a stay-at-home mom?" And my answer was "Yes!" First career, then stay-at-home mom, then a mix of the two, then back to career. I had an opportunity to have two careers *and* the family of my dreams—because we were in the fortunate position of not needing my income. There was also another reason whose full significance wouldn't become clear to me for years: I had the benefit of a small pill that allowed me to time and space my pregnancies.

It's a bit ironic, I think, that when Bill and I later began searching for ways to make a difference, I never drew a clear connection between our efforts to support the poorest people in the world and the contraceptives I was using to make the most of our family life. Family planning became part of our early giving, but we had a narrow understanding of its value, and I had no idea it was the cause that would bring me into public life.

Obviously, though, I understood the value of contraceptives for my own family. It's no accident that I didn't get pregnant until I had worked nearly a decade at Microsoft and Bill and I were ready to have children. It's no accident that Rory was born three years after Jenn, and our daughter Phoebe was born three years after Rory. It was my decision and Bill's to do it this way. Of course, there was luck involved, too. I was fortunate to be able to get pregnant when I wanted to. But I also had the ability to *not* get pregnant when I didn't want to. And that allowed us to have the life and family we wanted.

## Searching for a Huge Missed Idea

Bill and I formally set up the Bill & Melinda Gates Foundation in 2000. It was a merger of the Gates Learning Foundation and the William H. Gates Foundation. We named the foundation for both of us because I was going to have a big role in running it—more than Bill at the time, because he was still fully engaged at Microsoft and would be for the next eight years. At that point, we had two kids—Jenn was 4 and had started nursery school, and Rory was just 1—but I was excited to take on more work. I made it clear, however, that I wanted to work behind the scenes. I wanted to study the issues, take learning trips, and talk strategy—but for a long time I chose not to take a public role at the foundation. I saw what it was like for Bill to be out in the world and be well known, and that wasn't appealing to me. More important, though, I didn't want to spend more time away from the kids; I wanted to give them as normal an upbringing as possible. That was hugely important to me, and I knew that if I gave up my own privacy, it would be harder to protect the children's privacy. (When the kids started in school, we enrolled them with my family name, French, so they would have some anonymity.) Finally, I wanted to stay out of the public work because I'm a perfectionist. I've always felt I need to have an answer for every question, and I didn't feel I knew enough at that point to be a public voice for the foundation. So I made it clear I wouldn't make speeches or give interviews. That was Bill's job, at least at the start.

From the beginning, we were looking for problems that governments and markets weren't addressing or solutions they weren't trying. We wanted to discover the huge missed ideas that would allow a small investment to spark massive improvement. Our education began during our trip to Africa in 1993, the year before we were married. We hadn't established a foundation at that point, and we didn't have any idea how to invest money to improve people's lives.

But we saw scenes that stayed with us. I remember driving outside one of the towns and seeing a mother who was carrying a baby in her belly, another baby on her back, and a pile of sticks on her head. She had clearly been walking a long distance with no shoes, while the men I saw were wearing flip-flops and smoking cigarettes with no sticks on their heads or kids at their sides. As we drove on, I saw more women carrying heavy burdens, and I wanted to understand more about their lives.

After we returned from Africa, Bill and I hosted a small dinner at our home for Nan Keohane, then president of Duke University. I almost never hosted that kind of event back then, but I was glad I did. One researcher at the dinner told us about the huge number of children in poor countries who were dying from diarrhea and how oral rehydration salts could save their lives. Sometime after that, a colleague suggested we read *World Development Report 1993*. It showed that a huge number of deaths could be prevented with low-cost interventions, but the interventions weren't getting to people. Nobody felt it was their assignment. Then Bill and I read a heartbreaking article by Nicholas Kristof in *The New York Times* about diarrhea causing millions of childhood deaths in developing countries. Everything we heard and read had the same theme: Children in poor countries were dying from conditions that no kids died from in the United States.

Sometimes new facts and insights don't register until you hear them from several sources, and then everything starts coming together. As we kept reading about children who were dying whose lives could be saved, Bill and I began to think, *Maybe we can do something about this.*

The most bewildering thing to us was how little attention this got. In his speeches, Bill used the example of a plane crash. If a plane crashes, three hundred people die, and it's tragic for the families, and there's an article in every newspaper. But on the same day, thirty thousand children die, and that's tragic for the families, and there's no article in *any* newspaper. We didn't know about these children's deaths because they were happening in poor countries, and what's happening in poor countries doesn't get much attention in rich countries. That was the biggest shock to my conscience: Millions of children were dying because they were poor, and we weren't hearing about it because they were poor. That's when the work in global health started for us. We began to see how we could make an impact.

Saving children's lives was the goal that launched our global work, and our first big investment came in vaccines. We were horrified to learn that vaccines developed in the United States would take fifteen to twenty years to reach poor children in the developing world, and diseases that were killing kids in the developing world were not on the agenda of vaccine researchers back here. It was the first time we saw clearly what happens when there's no market incentive to serve poor children. Millions of kids die.

That was a crucial lesson for us, so we joined governments and other organizations to set up GAVI, the Vaccine Alliance, to use market mechanisms to help get vaccines to every child in the world. Another lesson we kept learning is that the problems of poverty and disease are always connected to each other. There are no isolated problems.

On one of my early trips for the foundation, I went to Malawi and was deeply moved to see so many mothers standing in long lines in the heat to get shots for their kids. When I talked to the women, they'd tell me the long distances they'd walked. Many had come ten or fifteen miles. They'd brought their food for the day. They'd had to bring not only the child who was getting vaccinated but their other children as well. It was a hard day for women whose whole lives were already hard. But it was a trip we were trying to make easier and shorter, and a trip we were urging more mothers to take.

I remember seeing a young mother with small kids and asking her, "Are you taking these beautiful children to get their shots?"

She answered, "What about *my* shot? Why do I have to walk twenty kilometers in this heat to get my shot?" She wasn't talking about a vaccination. She was talking about Depo-Provera, a long-acting birth control injection that could keep her from getting pregnant.

She already had more children than she could feed. She was afraid of having even more. But the prospect of spending a day walking with her children to a far-off clinic where her shot might not be in stock was deeply frustrating to her. She was just one of the many mothers I met during my early trips who switched the topic of our conversation from children's vaccines to family planning.

I remember traveling to a village in Niger and visiting a mother named Sadi Seyni whose six children were competing for her attention as we talked. She said the same thing I heard from so many mothers: "It wouldn't be fair for me to have another child. I can't afford to feed the ones I have now!"

In a large and very poor neighborhood of Nairobi named Korogocho I met Mary, a young mother who sold backpacks made from scraps of blue jean fabric. She invited me into her home, where she was sewing and watching her two small children. She used contraceptives because, she said, "Life is tough." I asked if her husband supported her decision. She said, "He knows life is tough, too."

Increasingly on my trips, no matter what their purpose, I began to hear and see the need for contraceptives. I visited communities where every mother had lost a child and everyone knew a mother who had died in childbirth. I met more mothers who were desperate not to get pregnant because they couldn't take care of the kids they already had. I began to understand why, even though I wasn't there to talk about contraceptives, women kept bringing them up anyway.

The women were experiencing in their lives what I was reading in the data.

In 2012, in the world's sixty-nine poorest countries, 260 million women were using contraceptives. Over 200 million more women in these nations wanted to use contraceptives—and couldn't get them. That meant millions of women in the developing world were getting pregnant too early, too late, and too often for their bodies to handle. When women in developing countries space their births by at least three years, each baby is almost twice as likely to survive their first year—and 35 percent more likely to see their fifth birthday. That's justification enough to expand access to contraceptives, but child survival is just one reason.

One of the longest-running public health studies dates from the 1970s, when half of the families in a number of villages in Bangladesh were given contraceptives and the other half were not. Twenty years later, the mothers who took contraceptives were healthier. Their children were better nourished. Their families had more wealth. The women had higher wages. Their sons and daughters had more schooling.

The reasons are simple: When the women were able to time and space their pregnancies, they were more likely to advance their education, earn an income, raise healthy children, and have the time and money to give each child the food, care, and education needed to thrive. When children reach their potential, they don't end up poor. This is how families and countries get out of poverty. In fact, no country in the last fifty years has emerged from poverty without expanding access to contraceptives.

We made contraception part of the early giving of our foundation, but our investment was not proportional to the benefits. It took us years to learn that contraceptives are the greatest life-saving, poverty-ending, women-empowering innovation ever created.

When we saw the full power of family planning, we knew that contraceptives had to be a higher priority for us.

It wasn't just a matter of writing bigger checks, either. We needed to fund new contraceptives that would have fewer side effects, last longer, and cost less, and that a woman could get in her own village or take by herself in her home. We needed a worldwide effort that included governments, global agencies, and drug companies working with local partners to deliver family planning to women where they lived. We needed a lot more voices speaking up for women who weren't being heard. By that time I had met many impressive people who had been working in the family planning movement for decades. I talked to as many as I could and asked them how our foundation could help, what I could do to amplify their voices.

Everyone I approached seemed to become awkwardly silent, as if the answer was obvious and I didn't see it. Finally, a few people told me, "The best way for you to support the public advocates is to become one. You need to join us."

That wasn't the answer I was looking for.

I am a private person—in certain ways, a bit shy. I was the girl in school who raised her hand to speak in class while other kids bellowed their answers from the back row. I like to work offstage. I want to study the data, go see the work, meet people, develop a strategy, and solve problems. By then, I was accustomed to making speeches and giving interviews. But suddenly friends, colleagues, and activists were pressing me to become a public advocate for family planning, and that alarmed me.

I thought, *Wow, am I going to step publicly into something as political as family planning, with my church and many conservatives so opposed to it?* When Patty Stonesifer was our foundation's CEO, she warned me, "Melinda, if the foundation ever steps into this space in a big way, you're going to be at the center of the controversy because you're Catholic. The questions will all be coming to you."

I knew this would be a huge shift for me. But it was clear the world had to do more on family planning. Despite decades of efforts by passionate advocates, progress had largely stalled. Family planning had fallen off as a global health priority. This was partly because it had become so politicized in the United States, and also because the AIDS epidemic and vaccine campaigns had drawn funding and attention away from contraceptives globally. (It is true that the AIDS epidemic did lead to widespread efforts to distribute condoms, but for reasons I'll explain later, condoms were not a helpful contraceptive tool for many women.)

I knew that my becoming an advocate for family planning would expose me to criticism I wasn't used to and would take time and energy from other foundation activities. But I began to feel that if anything was worth those costs, it was this. I felt it in a visceral, personal way. Family planning was indispensable to our ability to have a family. It allowed me to work and have the time to take care of each child. It was simple, cheap, safe, and powerful—no woman I knew went without it, but hundreds of millions of women around the world wanted it and couldn't get it. This unequal access was simply unjust. I couldn't look the other way as women and children were dying for want of a widely available tool that could save their lives.

I also considered my duty to my children. I had a chance to stand up for women who didn't have a voice. If I turned it down, what values was I role modeling for my kids? Would I want them to turn down difficult tasks in the future and then tell me that they were following my example?

And my own mother had a powerful influence on my choice, though she might not have known it. She always said to me as I was growing up, "If you don't set your own agenda, somebody else will." If I didn't fill my schedule with things I felt were important, other people would fill my schedule with things *they* felt were important.

Finally, I have always carried in my head images of the women I've met, and I keep photographs of the ones who have moved me the most. What was the point of their opening their hearts and telling me about their lives if I wasn't going to help them when I had the chance?

That clinched it for me. I decided to face my fears and speak out publicly for family planning.

I accepted an invitation from the UK government to cosponsor a family planning summit in London with as many heads of state, experts, and activists as we could attract. We decided we would double our foundation's commitment to family planning and make it a priority. We wanted to revive the global commitment that all women worldwide must have access to contraceptives, so that we can decide for ourselves whether and when to have a child.

But I still had to figure out what my role would be and what the foundation needed to do. It wouldn't be enough just to convene a global summit, talk about contraceptives, sign a declaration, and go home. We had to set goals and form a strategy.

We joined the UK government in a sprint to hold the summit in

London in July of 2012, two weeks before everyone's attention turned to the opening of the London Olympics at the end of the month.

The approach of the summit triggered a wave of media stories that highlighted the life-saving value of family planning. The British medical journal *The Lancet* published a study funded by the UK government and our foundation showing that access to contraception would cut the number of mothers who die in childbirth by a third. A report by Save the Children said a million teenage girls die or are injured in childbirth every year, which makes pregnancy the number one cause of death for teen girls. These findings and others helped set a tone of urgency for the conference.

There was a big crowd at the summit, including many heads of state. The speeches went well, and I was pleased with that. But I knew the test of success would be who stepped up and how much money we raised. What if national leaders didn't support the initiative? What if governments didn't increase their funding? Those worries had been giving me a sick feeling for months—not very different from the fear of throwing a party where no one shows up, but in this case, the media *would* show up to report on the failure.

I won't say that I shouldn't have worried. My worries make me work harder. But the funding and support were greater than my highest hopes. The United Kingdom doubled its commitment to family planning. The presidents of Tanzania, Rwanda, Uganda, and Burkina Faso and the vice president of Malawi were present at the conference and played a key role in raising the $2 billion committed by developing countries. That included Senegal, which doubled its commitment, and Kenya, which increased its national budget for family planning by a third. Together we pledged to make contraceptives available to 120 million more women by the end of the decade in a movement we called FP 2020. It was by far the largest sum of money ever pledged to support access to contraceptives.

## Just the Beginning

After the conference, my best friend from high school, Mary Lehman, who had traveled with me to London, joined me for dinner with some influential women who also attended the conference. We were all having a glass of wine and enjoying a sense of satisfaction, and I was personally relieved to be done. After many months of planning and worrying, I felt I could finally relax.

That's when these women all said to me, "Melinda, don't you see? Family planning is *just the first step* for women! We have to move on to a much bigger agenda!!"

I was the only one at the table naïve enough to be surprised—and I was *overwhelmed*. I didn't want to hear it. Talking to Mary in the car after dinner, I said over and over, "Mary, they've got to be kidding." I was near tears and kept thinking, *No way. I'm already doing my part and it's more than I can handle, and there is already a ton of work ahead on family planning alone to meet the goals we just declared—never mind a wider women's agenda.*

The call for "more" was especially hard to hear after an emotional visit I'd had a few days earlier in Senegal. I was sitting in a small hut with a group of women talking about female genital cutting. They had all been cut themselves. Many had held their daughters down to be cut. As they were telling me about it, my colleague Molly Melching, who's worked in Senegal for decades and was acting as my translator that day, said, "Melinda, some of this I'm not going to translate for you because I don't think you could take it." (At some point I have to summon the guts to ask her what she was holding back.)

Those women told me that they had all turned against the practice. When they were younger, they were afraid if they didn't have their daughters cut, the girls could never be married. When their daughters hemorrhaged to death, they believed it was evil spirits. But they had come to see these views as lies and had banned cutting in their village.

They believed they were telling me a story of progress, and they were. But to understand in what sense it was progress required an understanding of how cruel and widespread this practice still was. They were telling me how far they had come, and were also revealing to me how awful things still were for girls in their country. The story was horrifying to me—and I just shut down. I saw the effort as hopeless and endless, beyond my stamina and resources, and I said to myself, "I *quit*."

I suspect most of us, at one time or another, say "I quit." And we often find that "quitting" is just a painful step on the way to a deeper commitment. But I was still stuck in my private "I quit" from Senegal when the women at the table in London told me how much more had to be done. So I said my *second* "I quit" to myself in one week. I looked into the abyss between what needed to be done and what I was able to do and I just said "No!"

Even though I said it only to myself, I meant it. But later, when I began to drop my defenses, I realized that my "No!" was only a moment of rebellion before my surrender. I had to accept that the wounds of those girls in Senegal and the needs of women around the world were beyond anything I could heal. I had to accept that my job is to do my part, let my heart break for all the women we can't help, and stay optimistic.

Over time, I came to "Yes," and that allowed me to see what the women in London were telling me. Family planning was a first step, but that first step wasn't only gaining access to contraceptives; it was a step toward empowerment. Family planning means more than getting the right to decide whether and when to have children; it is the key to breaking through all kinds of barriers that have held women back for so long.

## My Huge Missed Idea: Invest in Women

Some years ago in India, I visited women's self-help groups and realized that I was seeing women empower each other. I was seeing women lifting each other up. And I saw that it all begins when women start talking to each other.

Over the years, the foundation has funded women's self-help groups with a number of different aims: to prevent the spread of HIV, to help women farmers buy better seeds, to help women get loans. There's a whole range of reasons to form groups. But no matter what the original focus, when women get information, tools, funding, and a sense of our power, women lift off and take the group where they want it to go.

In India, I met with women farmers in a self-help group who had purchased new seeds and were planting more crops and getting better yields on their farms—and they told me about it in the most personal ways. "Melinda, I used to live in a separate room in the house. I wasn't even allowed to be in the house with my mother-in-law. I had a room off the back, and I didn't have any soap. So I washed with ashes. But now I have money, so I can buy soap. And my sari is clean, and my mother-in-law respects me more. So she lets me in the house now. And I have more money now, and I bought my son a bike."

You want to talk about being respected by your mother-in-law? Buy your son a bike.

Why does this win respect? Not because of a local custom. It's universal. The mother-in-law respects the daughter-in-law because her income has improved the life of the family. When we women can use our talent and energy, we begin to speak in our own voices for our own values, and that makes everybody's life better.

As women gain rights, families flourish, and so do societies. That connection is built on a simple truth: Whenever you include a group that's been excluded, you benefit everyone. And when you're working globally to include women and girls, who are half of every population, you're working to benefit all members of *every* community. Gender equity lifts everyone.

From high rates of education, employment, and economic growth to low rates of teen births, domestic violence, and crime— the inclusion and elevation of women correlate with the signs of a healthy society. Women's rights and society's health and wealth rise together. Countries that are dominated by men suffer not only because they don't use the talent of their women but because they are run by men who have a need to exclude. Until they change their leadership or the views of their leaders, those countries will not flourish.

Understanding this link between women's empowerment and the wealth and health of societies is crucial for humanity. As much as any insight we've gained in our work over the past twenty years, this was our huge missed idea. *My* huge missed idea. If you want to lift up humanity, empower women. It is the most comprehensive, pervasive, high-leverage investment you can make in human beings.

I wish I could tell you the moment this insight came to me. I can't. It was like a slow-rising sun, gradually dawning on me—part of an awakening shared and accelerated by others, all of us coming to the same understanding and building momentum for change in the world.

One of my best friends, Killian Noe, has founded an organization called Recovery Café that serves people suffering from homelessness, addiction, and mental health challenges, and helps them build lives they're excited about living. Killian inspires me to explore things more deeply, and she has a question she's made famous among her friends: "What do you know now in a deeper way than you knew it before?" I love this question because it honors how we learn and grow. Wisdom isn't about accumulating more facts; it's about understanding big truths in a deeper way. Year by year, with the support and insight of friends and partners and people who have gone before me, I see more clearly that the primary causes of poverty and illness are the cultural, financial, and legal restrictions that block what women can do—*and think they can do*—for themselves and their children.

That's how women and girls became for me a point of leverage and a place to intervene across the range of barriers that keep people poor. The issues that make up the chapters in this book all have a gender focus: maternal and newborn health, family planning, women's and girls' education, unpaid work, child marriage, women in agriculture, women in the workplace. Each of these issues is shaped by barriers that block women's progress. When these barriers are broken, opportunities open up that not only lift women out of poverty, but can elevate women to equality with men in every culture and every level of society. No other single change can do more to improve the state of the world.

The correlation is as nearly perfect as any you will find in the world of data. If you search for poverty, you will find women who don't have power. If you explore prosperity, you will find women who do have power and use it.

When women can decide whether and when to have children; when women can decide whether and when and whom to marry; when women have access to healthcare, do only our fair share of unpaid labor, get the education we want, make the financial decisions we need, are treated with respect at work, enjoy the same rights as men, and rise up with the help of other women *and men* who train us in leadership and sponsor us for high positions—then women flourish . . . and our families and communities flourish with us.

We can look at each of these issues as a wall or a door. I think I already know which way we see it. In the hearts and minds of empowered women today, "every wall is a door."

Let's break down the walls and walk through the doors together.

# CHAPTER TWO

# Empowering Mothers

*Maternal and Newborn Health*

In 2016 on a trip to Europe, I made a special visit to Sweden to say good-bye to one of my heroes.

Hans Rosling, who died in 2017, was a trailblazing professor of international health who became famous for teaching experts facts they should already know. He became well known for his unforgettable TED Talks (more than 25 million views and counting); for his book *Factfulness,* written with his son and daughter-in-law, which shows us that the world is better than we think it is; and for their Gapminder Foundation, whose original work with data and graphics has helped people see the world as it is. For me personally, Hans was a wise mentor whose stories helped me see poverty through the eyes of the poor.

I want to tell you a story Hans shared with me that helped me see the impact of extreme poverty—and how empowering women can play the central role in ending it.

First, though, I should let you know that Hans Rosling was less taken with me than I was with him, at least at the start. In 2007, before we knew each other, he came to an event where I was going to speak. He was skeptical, he later told me. He was thinking, *American billionaires giving away money will mess everything up!* (He wasn't wrong to be worried. More on that later.)

I won him over, he said, because in my remarks I didn't talk about sitting back in Seattle reading data and developing theories. Instead, I tried to share what I'd learned from the midwives, nurses, and mothers I had met during my trips to Africa and South Asia. I told stories about women farmers who left their fields to walk for miles to a health clinic and endured a long, hot wait in line only to be told that contraceptives were out of stock. I talked about midwives who said their pay was low, their training slight, and they had no ambulances. I purposely didn't go into these visits with fixed views; I tried to go with curiosity and a desire to learn. So did Hans, it turns out, and he started much earlier than I did and with greater intensity.

When Hans was a young doctor, he and his wife, Agneta—who was a distinguished healthcare professional in her own right—moved to Mozambique, where Hans practiced medicine in a poor region far from the capital. He was one of two doctors responsible for 300,000 people. They were all his patients, in his view, even if he never saw them—and usually he didn't. His district had 15,000 births a year and more than 3,000 childhood deaths. Every day in his district, ten children died. Hans treated diarrhea, malaria, cholera, pneumonia, and problem births. When there are two doctors for 300,000 people, you treat everything.

This experience shaped who he was and defined what he taught me. After we met, Hans and I never attended the same event without getting time with each other, even if it was only a few minutes in the hallway between sessions. In our visits—some long, some short—he became my teacher. Hans not only helped me learn about extreme poverty; he helped me look back and better understand what I had already seen. "Extreme poverty produces diseases," he said. "Evil forces hide there. It's where Ebola starts. It's where Boko Haram hides girls." It took me a long time to learn what he knew, even when I had the advantage of learning it from him.

Nearly 750 million people are living in extreme poverty now, down from 1.85 billion people in 1990. According to the policymakers, people in extreme poverty are those living on the equivalent of $1.90 a day. But those numbers don't capture the desperation of their lives. What extreme poverty really means is that no matter how hard you work, you're trapped. You can't get out. Your efforts barely matter. You've been left behind by those who could lift you up. That's what Hans helped me understand.

Over the course of our friendship, he would always say, "Melinda, you have to be about the people on the margins." So we tried together to see life through the eyes of the people we hoped to serve. I told him about my first foundation trip and how I came away with so much respect for the people I saw because I knew their daily reality would ruin me.

I had visited the slum of a large city, and what shocked me was not little kids coming up to the car and begging. I expected that. It was seeing little kids fending for themselves. It shouldn't have surprised me; it's the obvious consequence of poor mothers having no choice but to go off to work. It's a matter of survival in the city. But whom do they leave the baby with? I saw children walking around with infants. I saw a 5-year-old running with his friends in the street, carrying a baby who was still in the wobbly-headed stage. I saw kids playing near electrical wires on a rooftop and running near sewage that was streaming down the edge of the street. I saw children playing near pots of boiling water where vendors were cooking the food they were selling. The danger was part of the kids' day and part of their reality. It couldn't be changed by a mother making a better choice—the mothers had no better choice to make. They had to work, and they were doing the best anyone could do in that situation to take care of their kids. I had so much regard for them, for their ability to keep on doing what they had to do to feed their children. I talked many times with Hans about what I saw, and I think it prompted him to tell me what *he* saw. The story Hans shared with me a few months before he died was, he told me, the one that he thought best captured the essence of poverty.

When Hans was a doctor in Mozambique in the early 1980s, there was a cholera epidemic in the district where he worked. Each day he would go out with his small staff in his health service jeep to find the people with cholera rather than wait for them to come to him.

One day they drove into a remote village at sunset. There

were about fifty houses there, all made of mud blocks. The people had cassava fields and some cashew nut trees but no donkeys, cows, or horses—and no transportation to get their produce to market.

As Hans's team arrived, a crowd peered inside his jeep and began saying, *"Doutor Comprido, Doutor Comprido,"* which in Portuguese means "Doctor Tall, Doctor Tall." That's how Hans was known—never "Doctor Rosling" or "Doctor Hans," just "Doctor Tall." Most of the villagers had never seen him before, but they had heard of him. Now Doctor Tall had come to their village, and as he got out of the car, he asked the village leaders, *"Fala português?"* Do you speak Portuguese? *"Poco, poco,"* they answered. A little. *"Bem vindo, Doutor Comprido."* Welcome, Doctor Tall.

So Hans asked, "How do you know me?"

"Oh, you are very well known in this village."

"But I've never been here before."

"No, you've never been here. That's why we are so happy you've come. We are very happy." Others joined in: "He is welcome, he is welcome, Doctor Tall."

More and more people gathered, joining the crowd softly. Soon there were fifty people around, smiling and looking at Doctor Tall.

"But there are very few people from this village who come to my hospital," Hans said.

"No, we very seldom go to hospital."

"So how come you know me?"

"Oh, you are respected. You are so respected."

"I am respected? But I've never been here."

"No, you've never been here. And yes, very few go to your

hospital, but one woman came to your hospital, and you treated her. So you are very respected."

"Ah! One woman from this village?"

"Yes, one of our women."

"Why did she come?"

"Problem with childbirth."

"So she came to be treated?"

"Yes, and you are so respected because you treated her."

Hans started feeling a bit of pride, and asked, "Can I see her?"

"No," everyone said. "No, you cannot see her."

"Why not? Where is she?"

"She's dead."

"Oh, I'm sorry. She died?"

"Yes, she died when you treated her."

"You said this woman had a problem giving birth?"

"Yes."

"And who took her to the hospital?"

"Her brothers."

"And she came to the hospital?"

"Yes."

"And I treated her?"

"Yes."

"And then she died?"

"Yes, she died on the table where you treated her."

Hans began to get nervous. Did they think he'd blundered? Were they about to unleash their grief on him? He glanced to see if his driver was in the car so he could make a getaway. He saw it was impossible to run so he began to talk slowly and softly.

"So, what illness did the woman have? I don't remember her."

"Oh, you must remember her, you must remember her, because the arm of the child came out. The midwife tried to drag the child out by the arm, but it was impossible."

(This, Hans explained to me, is called an arm presentation. It blocks the chance of getting the child out because of the position of the baby's head.)

At that point, Hans remembered everything. The child was dead when they arrived. He had to remove the child to save the life of the mother. A C-section was never an option; Hans didn't have the setting for surgery. So he attempted a fetotomy (bringing out the dead infant in pieces), and the uterus ruptured and the mother bled to death on the operating table. Hans couldn't stop it.

"Yes, it was very sad," Hans said. "Very sad. I tried to save her by cutting off the baby's arm."

"Yes, you cut off the arm."

"Yes, I cut off the arm. I tried to take the body out in pieces."

"Yes, you tried to take it out in pieces. That's what you told the brothers."

"I'm very, very sorry that she died."

"Yes, so are we. We are very sorry, she was a good woman," they said.

Hans exchanged courtesies with them, and when there wasn't much else to say, he asked—because he is curious and courageous—"But how can I be respected when I didn't save the woman's life?"

"Oh, we knew it was difficult. We know that most women who have the arm coming out will die. We knew that it was difficult."

"But why did you respect me?"

"Because of what you did afterward."

"What was that?"

"You went out of the room into your yard. You stopped the vaccination car from leaving. You ran to catch up with it, you made the car come back, you took out boxes from the car, and you arranged for the woman from our village to be wrapped in a white sheet. You provided the sheet, and you even provided a small sheet for the pieces of the baby. Then you arranged for the woman's body to be put into that jeep, and you made one of your staff get out so there would be room for the brothers to go with her. So after that tragedy, she was back home the same day while the sun was still shining. We had the funeral that evening, and her whole family, everyone was here. We never expected anyone to show such respect for us poor farmers here in the forest. You are deeply respected for what you do. Thank you very much. You will always be in our memory."

Hans paused here in the story and told me, "I wasn't the one who did that. It was Mama Rosa."

Mama Rosa was a Catholic nun who worked with Hans. She had told him, "Before you do a fetotomy, get permission from the family. Don't cut a baby before you have their permission. Afterward, they will ask you only for one thing, to get the parts of the child. And you will say, 'Yes, you will get the parts, and you will be given the cloth for the child.' That's the way. They don't want anybody else to have parts of their baby. They want to see all the pieces."

So Hans explained, "When this woman died, I was sobbing, and Mama Rosa put her arm around me and said, 'This woman was from a very remote village. We must take her home. Otherwise no one will come to the hospital from that village for the next decade.'

"'But how can we take her?'

"'Run out and stop the vaccine car,' Mama Rosa told me. 'Run out and stop the vaccine car.'"

And Hans did it. "Mama Rosa knew what people's realities were," he said. "I never would have known to do that. Often in life, it's the older males who get credit for the work that young people and women do. It isn't right, but that's how it works."

That was Hans's deepest witness of extreme poverty. It wasn't living on a dollar a day. It was taking days to get to the hospital when you're dying. It was respecting a doctor not for saving a life but for returning a dead body to the village.

If this mother had lived in a prosperous community and not on the margins among farmers in a remote forest in Mozambique, she never would have lost her baby. She never would have lost her life.

This is the meaning of poverty I've come to see in my work, and I see it also in Hans's story: Poverty is not being able to protect your family. Poverty is not being able to save your children when mothers with more money could. And because the strongest instinct of a mother is to protect her children, poverty is the most disempowering force on earth.

It follows that if you want to attack poverty and if you want to empower women, you can do both with one approach: *Help mothers protect their children*. That is how Bill and I began our philanthropic work. We didn't put it in those words at the time. It just struck us as the most unjust thing in the world for children to die because their parents are poor.

In late 1999, in our first global initiative, we joined with countries and organizations to save the lives of children under 5. A huge part of the campaign was expanding worldwide coverage for a basic package of vaccines, which had helped cut the number of childhood deaths in half since 1990, from 12 million a year to 6 million.

Unfortunately, the survival rate of newborns—babies in the first twenty-eight days of life—has not improved at the same pace. Of all the deaths of children under 5, nearly half come in the first month. And of all the deaths in the first month, the greatest number come on the first day. These babies are born to the poorest of the poor—many in places far beyond the reach of hospitals. How can you save millions of babies when their families are spread out in remote areas and follow centuries of tradition when it comes to childbirth?

We didn't know. But if we wanted to do the most good, we had to go where there's the most harm—so we explored ways to save the lives of mothers and newborn babies. The most common factor in maternal and infant death is the lack of skilled providers. Forty million women a year give birth without assistance. We found that the best response—at least the best response we have the know-how to deliver now—is to train and deploy more skilled healthcare providers to be present for mothers at birth and in the hours and days after.

In 2003, we funded the work of Vishwajeet Kumar, a medical doctor with advanced training from Johns Hopkins who was launching a life-saving program in a village called Shivgarh in Uttar Pradesh, one of India's poorest states.

In the midst of this project, Vishwajeet married a woman named Aarti Singh. Aarti was an expert in bioinformatics—and began applying her expertise to designing and evaluating programs for mothers and newborns. She became an indispensable member of the organization, which was named Saksham, or "empowerment," by the people in the village.

Vishwajeet and the Saksham team had studied births in poor rural parts of India and saw that there were many common practices that were high risk for the baby. They believed that many newborn deaths could be prevented with practices that cost little or nothing and could be done by the community: immediate breastfeeding, keeping the baby warm, cutting the cord with sterilized tools. It was just a matter of changing behavior. With grants from USAID and Save the Children and our foundation—and by teaching safe newborn practices to community health workers—Saksham cut newborn mortality in half in eighteen months.

At the time of my 2010 visit to Shivgarh, there were still 3 million newborn deaths in the world every year. Nearly 10 percent of those deaths occurred in Uttar Pradesh, which has been called the global epicenter of newborn and maternal deaths. If you wanted to bring down the number of newborn deaths, Uttar Pradesh was an important place to work.

On the first day of my trip, I met with about a hundred people from the village to talk about newborn care. It was a large crowd, with mothers seated at the front and men toward the back. But it felt intimate. We were sitting on rugs laid out under the shade of a large tree, packed in tightly to make sure no one was left out in the blistering sun. After the meeting, we were greeted by a family with a little boy about 6 years old. Seconds later, Gary Darmstadt, who was our foundation's head of maternal and newborn health at the time, whispered to me, "That was *him*; that was the baby!" I looked back and saw the 6-year-old boy and said, "What baby? That's not a baby." "That's the one Ruchi saved," he said. "Oh my gosh!" I said. "That's the baby you told me about!?"

That 6-year-old boy had become lore. He was born in the first month of the Saksham program when the community health workers had just been trained, community skepticism was high, and everyone was watching. The baby, whom I had just seen as a healthy 6-year-old, was born in the middle of the night. The mother, in her first pregnancy, was exhausted and fainted during childbirth.

As soon as the sun came up, the recently trained community health worker was notified of the birth and came immediately. Her name was Ruchi. She was about 20 years old and came from a high-caste Indian family. When she arrived, she found the mother still unconscious and the baby cold. Ruchi asked what was going on, and none of the family members in the room said a thing. They were all terrified.

Ruchi stoked the fire to warm the room, then got blankets and wrapped the baby. She took the baby's temperature—because she was trained to know that hypothermia can kill babies or be a sign of infection. The infant was extremely cold, about 94 degrees. So Ruchi tried the conventional things she'd done in the past, and nothing worked. The baby was turning blue. He was listless, and Ruchi realized that he would die unless she did something right away.

One of the life-saving practices Ruchi had learned was skin-to-skin care: holding a baby against the mother's skin to transfer warmth from the mom to the newborn. The technique prevents hypothermia. It promotes breastfeeding. It protects from infection. It is one of the most powerful interventions we know of for saving babies.

Ruchi asked the baby's aunt to give the infant skin-to-skin care, but the aunt refused. She was afraid that the evil spirit she thought was gripping the baby would take her over as well.

Ruchi then faced a choice: Would she give the baby skin-to-skin care herself? The decision wasn't easy; doing something so intimate with a low-caste infant could bring ridicule from her own relatives. And this was a foreign practice in the community. If it didn't go well, the family could blame her for the death of the baby.

But when she saw the baby getting colder, she opened up her sari and placed the newborn against her bare skin, with the baby's head nestled between her breasts and a cloth covering both her head and the baby's for modesty and warmth. Ruchi held the baby that way for a couple of minutes. His skin color appeared to be changing back to pink. She took out her thermometer and tested the baby's temperature. A little better. She held the baby a few minutes more and took his temperature again. A little bit higher. Every woman there leaned in and watched as the baby's temperature rose. A few minutes later, the baby started to move; then he came alive; then he started to cry. The baby was fine. He wasn't infected. He was just a healthy baby who needed to be warmed and hugged.

When the mother regained consciousness, Ruchi told her what had happened and guided her in skin-to-skin care, then helped her initiate breastfeeding. Ruchi stayed another hour or so, watching the mother and baby in skin-to-skin position, and then she left the home.

This story spread like lightning through the nearby villages.

Overnight, women went from saying "We're not sure about this practice" to "I want to do this for my baby." It was a turning point in the project. You don't get behavior change unless a new practice is transparent, works well, and gets people talking—and Ruchi's revival of this one-day-old baby had everybody talking. This was a practice all women could do. Mothers became seen as life-savers. It was immensely empowering and transformative.

## Their Cup Is Not Empty

I learned a lot from my trip to Shivgarh, and the most striking lesson for me—and what made it a departure from a lot of our prior work—is that it wasn't about technological advances. Our emphasis at the foundation has always been on scientific research to develop life-saving breakthroughs like vaccines. We call this product development, and it continues to be our main contribution. But Vishwa-jeet and Aarti's program for mothers and newborns showed me how much can be achieved by sharing simple practices that are widely known throughout the world. This taught me in a profound way that you have to understand human needs in order to effectively deliver services and solutions to people. Delivery systems matter.

What do I mean by a "delivery system"? Getting tools to people who need them in ways that encourage people to use them—*that* is a delivery system. It is crucial, and it is often complex. It can require getting around barriers of poverty, distance, ignorance, doubt, stigma, and religious and gender bias. It means listening to people, learning what they want, what they're doing, what they believe, and what barriers they face. It means paying attention to how people live their lives. That's what you need to do if you have a life-saving tool or technique you want to deliver to people.

Before launching the program, Saksham hired a local team of top students who spent six months working with the community to understand their existing practices and beliefs around childbirth. Vishwajeet told me, "Their cup is not empty; you can't just pour your ideas into it. Their cup is already full, so you have to understand what is in their cup." If you don't understand the meaning and beliefs behind a community's practices, you won't present your idea in the context of their values and concerns, and people won't hear you.

Historically, the mothers in the community would go to the Brahmin, a member of the priestly caste, and ask when to start breastfeeding, and he would say, "You can't let down milk for three days, so you should start after three days." False information is disempowering. Mothers would heed the advice of the Brahmin, and for the first three days of the newborn's life, they would give the baby water—which was often polluted. Vishwajeet and Aarti's team had prepared for this moment. They gently questioned traditional practices by pointing to patterns in nature that were part of the villagers' way of life. They cited the example of a calf and its mother. "When we try to milk a cow and it doesn't express milk, we make the calf suckle her to get the milk to let down, so why don't you try the same and keep the baby against your breast to express milk."

The villagers still said, "No, this isn't going to work." So the local team went to a few people in the community who had courage and influence and tried to persuade them. Team members knew that if they could create a culture of support around a young mother, the mother would be much more likely to try the new practice. When a few mothers tried it and were able to breastfeed right away, they said, "Wait a minute; we didn't realize we could do this!" Then things took off; the community began to try the other health practices as well.

It's a delicate thing to initiate change in a traditional culture. It has to be done with the utmost care and respect. Transparency is crucial. Grievances must be heard. Failures must be acknowledged. Local people have to lead. Shared goals have to be emphasized. Messages have to appeal to people's experience. The practice has to work clearly and quickly, and it's important to emphasize the science. If love were enough to save a life, no mother would ever bury her baby—we need the science as well. But the way you deliver the science is just as important as the science itself.

## Midwife in Every Village

When I returned to the foundation after my trip to Shivgarh, I talked to our staff about delivery and cultural awareness and how crucial they are to saving lives. I said we have to keep working on innovation in products, in science and technology, but we have to work with the same passion on innovation in delivery systems as well. Both are indispensable.

Let me illustrate with an example that is personal to me, and one I haven't shared before. It's about my mom's older sister Myra.

My aunt Myra is very dear to me. I called her "my other mother" when I was growing up. When she used to visit us, she would spend time coloring and playing board games with my sister, Susan, and me. We also went shopping a lot. She was so energetic and upbeat that it didn't ever figure in my image of Aunt Myra that she didn't have the use of her legs.

When my mom and Myra were young girls in the 1940s, they were playing at their great-uncle's house, and afterward he told my grandmother, "Myra was sure being lazy today. She wanted me to carry her home."

That night Myra woke up screaming in pain. My grandparents took her to the hospital, and a team of doctors figured out she had polio. They wrapped her legs up with gauze, boiled water, and put on hot packs. Doctors thought the heat would help, but it didn't make any difference. Three or four days later, her legs were paralyzed. She was in the hospital for sixteen months, and my grandparents were allowed to visit her only on Sundays. Meanwhile, none of the kids in the neighborhood would play with my mom anymore. Everyone was terrified of the polio virus.

In the 1940s, the great polio challenge was product development, namely, finding a vaccine. Delivery didn't matter. There was nothing to deliver. It wasn't a question of privilege or poverty. The scientific innovation hadn't happened yet. There was no protection for anyone against polio.

As soon as Jonas Salk developed his polio vaccine in 1953, the passionate effort to protect people from polio shifted from product development to delivery, and in this case, poverty did matter. People in wealthy countries were vaccinated quickly. By the late 1970s, polio had been eliminated in the US, but it continued to plague much of the world, including India, where the vast landscapes and large population made polio especially hard to fight. In 2011, defying most expert predictions, India became polio free. It was one of the greatest accomplishments in global health, and India did it with an army of more than 2 million vaccinators who traversed the entire country to find and vaccinate every child.

In March of 2011, Bill and I met a young mother and her family in a small village in Bihar, one of the most rural states in India. They were migrant workers, desperately poor, and working at a brick kiln. We asked her if her children had been vaccinated for polio, and she went into her hut and returned with an immunization card with the names of her children and the dates they received the vaccine. The vaccinators had not just found her children once. They had done so several times. We were awestruck. That is how India became polio free—through massive, heroic, original, and ingenious delivery.

Meeting people who deliver life-saving support to others is one of the highlights of my work. A few years ago on a trip to Indonesia, I met a woman named Ati Pujiastuti. As a young woman, Ati had enrolled in a government program called Midwife in Every Village that trained 60,000 midwives. She completed the program when she was just 19 years old and was assigned to work in a rural mountain village.

When she arrived in the village, she wasn't welcome. People were hostile and distrustful of outsiders, especially young women with ideas for how to make things better. Somehow, this young woman had the wisdom of a village elder. She went door-to-door to introduce herself to everyone. She showed up at every community event. She bought the local newspaper and read it aloud to anyone who couldn't read. When the village got electricity, she scraped up the money to buy a tiny TV and invited everyone to come watch with her.

Still, nobody wanted her services until, by pure accident, a pregnant woman who was visiting the village from Jakarta went into labor and asked Ati to deliver her baby. The birth went well, the villagers began to trust Ati, and soon every family wanted her present when mothers gave birth. She made sure that she was there, every time, even at the risk of her own life. Once she lost her footing while crossing a river and had to cling to a rock until help came. Another time she slipped on a muddy mountain path next to the edge of a cliff. Several times, she was thrown off her motorbike while riding on unpaved roads. Still, she stayed on and kept delivering babies. She knew she was saving lives.

As much as we need women on the ground delivering these services, we also need women in high places with vision and power. One of those women is Dr. Agnes Binagwaho, the former health minister of Rwanda.

In 2014, Agnes and I coauthored a piece in *The Lancet*. We called attention to the newborn lives that could be saved if the world could remedy one harsh reality: Most women in low-income countries give birth at home without a skilled attendant.

Putting a skilled birth attendant at the side of every mother in labor has been one of the great causes of Agnes's life.

It's not a cause anyone would have predicted twenty-five years ago. Agnes was working as a pediatrician in Europe in 1994 when she began hearing frightening news reports from home. Members of the majority ethnic group, the Hutus, had begun slaughtering minority Tutsis. She followed the horror from afar as almost a million people were murdered in a hundred days. Half of her husband's family was killed.

Agnes hadn't lived in Rwanda since she was 3 years old, when her father moved the family to France so he could go to medical school. But after the genocide, she and her husband decided to return to their country and help rebuild.

Returning to Rwanda was a shock, especially for a medical doctor who practiced in Europe. Even before the genocide, Rwanda was one of the worst places in the world to give birth, and the conflict made the situation far worse. Almost all the nation's health workers had either fled or been killed, and wealthy nations weren't giving health aid. A week after she arrived, Agnes nearly left. But her heart was breaking for those who couldn't leave—so she stayed, became the longest-serving health minister in her country's history, and spent the next two decades helping to build a new health system for Rwanda.

Under Agnes, the health ministry started a program where each Rwandan village (with about 300 to 450 residents) elects three community health workers—one dedicated solely to maternal health.

These and other changes have been dramatically successful. Since the genocide, Rwanda has made more progress in making birth safer than almost any other nation in the world. Newborn mortality is down by 64 percent. Maternal mortality is down by 77 percent. A generation after Rwanda was considered a lost cause, its health system is studied as a model. Agnes is now working with Dr. Paul Farmer, one of my heroes for bringing healthcare to poor people, first in Haiti and then around the world. Partners in Health, which Paul cofounded, has launched a new health sciences university in Rwanda, the University of Global Health Equity. Agnes is vice-chancellor of the university and is promoting fresh research into what makes delivery work.

What inspires me most about Agnes's work in Rwanda, Ati's work in Indonesia, and Vishwajeet and Aarti's work in India is that they all show how a passionate emphasis on delivering services can ease the effects of poverty. This underscores the value of Hans Rosling's stories about extreme poverty: When you begin to understand the daily lives of the poor, it does more than give you the desire to help; it can often show you how.

When people are not getting healthcare that most others get, the problem is by definition one of delivery. Medicine, services, and skilled assistance are not reaching them. That's what it means to be poor. They're on the margins. They're not getting the benefit of what human beings know how to do for each other. So we have to invent a way of getting it to them. This is what it means to fight the effects of poverty. It's unglamorous from a technological standpoint, but deeply satisfying from a human viewpoint—innovation driven by the feeling that science should serve everyone. No one should be excluded.

That is a lesson I have kept close to my heart: Poverty is created by barriers; we have to get around or break down those barriers to deliver solutions. But that's not all. The more I saw our work in the field, the more I realized that delivery needs to shape strategy. The challenge of delivery reveals the causes of poverty. You learn *why* people are poor. You don't have to *guess* what the barriers are. As soon as you try to deliver help, you run into them.

When a mother can't get what she needs to protect her children, it's not just that she's poor. It's something more precise. She doesn't have access to a skilled birth attendant with the latest knowledge and crucial health tools. Why? There could be many reasons. She doesn't have information. She doesn't have money. She lives far from town. Her husband is opposed to it. Her mother-in-law doubts it. She doesn't think she can ask for it. Her culture frowns on it. When you know why a mother can't get what she needs, you can figure out what to do.

If the barrier is distance, money, knowledge, or stigma, we have to offer tools and information that are closer, cheaper, and less tainted by stigma. To fight poverty, we have to see and study the barriers and figure out if they're cultural, or social, or economic, or geographic, or political, and then go around them or through them so the poor aren't cut off from benefits others enjoy.

As soon as we began to spend more time understanding how people live their lives, we saw that so many of the barriers to advancement—and so many of the causes of isolation—can be traced to the limits put on the lives of women.

In societies of deep poverty, women are pushed to the margins. Women are outsiders. That's not a coincidence. When any community pushes any group out, especially its women, it's creating a crisis that can only be reversed by bringing the outsiders back in. This is the core remedy for poverty and almost any social ill—including the excluded, going to the margins of society and bringing everybody back in.

Back when I was in elementary school, there were two girls who sat at the back of the class, smart girls, but quiet and a little socially awkward. And there were two other girls, socially confident and popular, who sat toward the front of the class. The popular girls in front picked on the quiet girls in the back. I'm not talking about once a week. It was constant.

They were careful to do it when the teacher couldn't see or hear—so no one did anything to stop them. And the quiet girls just got quieter. They were afraid to look up and make eye contact because it would bring on more abuse. They suffered terribly, and the pain never went away even after the bullying stopped. Decades later, at a class reunion, one of the popular girls apologized, and one of the girls who was bullied answered, "It's about time you said something."

All of us have seen something like this. And we all had a role in it. Either we were bullies, or we were victims, or we saw bullying and didn't stop it. I was in that last group. I saw everything I just described. And I didn't stop it because I was afraid that if I spoke up, the bullies would turn on me too. I wish I had known how to find my voice and help the other girls find theirs.

As I grew up, I thought abuse like that would happen less and less. But I was wrong. Adults try to create outsiders, too. In fact, we get better at it. And most of us fall into one of the same three groups: the people who try to create outsiders, the people who are made to feel like outsiders, and the people who stand by and don't stop it.

Anyone can be made to feel like an outsider. It's up to the people who have the power to exclude. Often it's on the basis of race. Depending on a culture's fears and biases, Jews can be treated as outsiders. Muslims can be treated as outsiders. Christians can be treated as outsiders. The poor are always outsiders. The sick are often outsiders. People with disabilities can be treated as outsiders. Members of the LGBTQ community can be treated as outsiders. Immigrants are almost always outsiders. And in most every society, women can be made to feel like outsiders—even in their own homes.

Overcoming the need to create outsiders is our greatest challenge as human beings. It is the key to ending deep inequality. We stigmatize and send to the margins people who trigger in us the feelings we want to avoid. This is why there are so many old and weak and sick and poor people on the margins of society. We tend to push out the people who have qualities we're most afraid we will find in ourselves—and sometimes we falsely ascribe qualities we disown to certain groups, then push those groups out as a way of denying those traits in ourselves. This is what drives dominant groups to push different racial and religious groups to the margins.

And we're often not honest about what's happening. If we're on the inside and see someone on the outside, we often say to ourselves, "I'm not in that situation because I'm *different*." But that's just pride talking. We could *easily* be that person. We have all things inside us. We just don't like to confess what we have in common with outsiders because it's too humbling. It suggests that maybe success and failure aren't entirely fair. And if you know you got the better deal, then you have to be humble, and it hurts to give up your sense of superiority and say, "I'm no better than others." So instead we invent excuses for our need to exclude. We say it's about merit or tradition when it's really just protecting our privilege and our pride.

In Hans's story, the mother from the forest lost her life because she was an outsider. She lost her baby because she was an outsider.

And her family had a warm memory of the doctor who returned their bodies to the village because they were outsiders. They were not used to being treated with respect. That is why they suffered so much death.

Saving lives starts with bringing everyone in. Our societies will be healthiest when they have no outsiders. We should strive for that. We have to keep working to reduce poverty and disease. We have to help outsiders resist the power of people who want to keep them out. But we have to do our inner work as well: We have to wake up to the ways we exclude. We have to open our arms and our hearts to the people we've pushed to the margins. It's not enough to help outsiders fight their way in—the real triumph will come when we no longer push anyone out.

CHAPTER THREE

# Every Good Thing

*Family Planning*

A few days after I visited Vishwajeet and Aarti's program, which trained community health workers who attended home births, I visited a maternal and newborn health program called Sure Start, which encourages mothers to deliver in clinics with trained birth attendants and medical equipment.

When I arrived at the project site, I was invited to watch a group of twenty-five pregnant women playing a quiz game on principles of good health, answering questions about early breastfeeding and first-hour newborn care. Then I met with a women's group centered on pregnant women and their family members, mainly mothers-in-law and sisters-in-law. I asked the pregnant women if they faced any family resistance for participating in the program. Then I asked the mothers-in-law what changes they'd seen since they'd been pregnant with their own children. One older woman told me that she had given birth to eight children at home, but six had died within a week of delivery. Her daughter-in-law was now pregnant for the first time, and the older woman wanted her to receive the best possible care.

In the afternoon, I was able to visit the home of a mother named Meena who had delivered a baby boy just two weeks before. Meena's husband worked for daily wages near their home. Their children had all been delivered at home except for the newborn, who was born in a clinic with the support of Sure Start. Meena held her infant in her arms as we talked.

I asked Meena if the program had helped her, and she gave me an enthusiastic yes. She felt delivering in a clinic was safer for her and the baby, and she had started breastfeeding the same day, which made her feel free to bond with her baby immediately, and she loved that. She was very animated, very positive. She clearly felt good about the program, and therefore so did I.

Then I asked her, "Do you want to have any more children?"

She looked as if I'd shouted at her. She cast her eyes down and stayed silent for an awkwardly long time. I was worried that I'd said something rude, or maybe the interpreter had offered a bad translation, because Meena kept staring at the ground. Then she raised her head, looked me in the eyes, and said, "The truth is no, I don't want to have any more kids. We're very poor. My husband works hard, but we're just extremely poor. I don't know how I'm going to feed this child. I have no hopes for educating him. In fact, I have no hopes for this child's future at all."

I was stunned. People tend to tell me the good news, and I often have to ask probing questions to find out the rest. This woman had the courage to tell me the whole painful truth. I didn't have to ask. And she wasn't finished.

"The only hope I have for this child's future," she said, "is if you'll take him home with you." Then she put her hand on the head of the 2-year-old boy at her leg and said, "Please take him, too."

I was *reeling*. In a moment, we had gone from a joyous conversation about a healthy birth to a dark confession about a mother's suffering—suffering so great that the pain of giving her babies away was less than the pain of keeping them.

When a woman shares her grief with me, I see it as a huge honor. I listen intently, offer sympathy, and then try to point out an upside somewhere. But if I had tried in that moment to say something upbeat to Meena, it would have been false and offensive. I asked her a question and she told me the truth; it would have denied her pain to pretend to be positive. And the pain she described was beyond anything I could imagine—she felt the only way to help her children live a good life was to find them another mother.

I told her as gently as I could that I had three children of my own, and that her children loved her and needed her. Then I asked, "Do you know about family planning?" She said, "I do now, but you people didn't tell me before, and now it's too late for me."

This young mother felt like a complete failure, and so did I. We had totally let her down. I was so overwhelmed with emotion, I don't even recall how we parted or how I said good-bye.

Meena dominated my mind for the rest of the trip. It took me a long time before I could take it all in. Clearly, it was good to help her deliver in a facility, but it wasn't good enough. We weren't seeing the whole picture. We had a maternal and newborn health program, and we talked to expecting mothers about their needs in maternal and newborn health. That was the lens we looked through to see the work, but the lenses we *should* have been looking through were the eyes of Meena.

When I talk to women in low-income countries, I see very little difference in what we women all want for ourselves and our children. We want our kids to be safe, to be healthy, to be happy, to do well in school, to fulfill their potential, to grow up and have families and livelihoods of their own—to love and be loved. And we want to be healthy ourselves and develop our own gifts and share them with the community.

Family planning is important in meeting every one of those needs, no matter where a woman lives. It took a woman with courage to burn this message into me, and her pain became a turning point in my work. When one person tells me a harsh truth, I can be sure that she's speaking for others who aren't as bold. It makes me pay better attention, and then I realize that others have been saying the same thing all along, just more softly. I haven't heard it because I haven't really been listening.

Shortly after I spoke to Meena, I traveled to Malawi and paid a visit to a health center. The center had a room for vaccinations, a room for sick kids, a room for HIV patients, and a room for family planning. There was a long line of women waiting to visit the family planning room, and I talked to a few of them—asking where they had come from, how many children they had, when they started using contraceptives, what kind of contraceptives they used. My nosiness was matched by the women's eagerness to talk about their lives. One woman told me that she had come to get her injection but didn't know if it would be available, and all the other women nodded. They said they would walk ten miles to the health clinic not knowing if the shot would be in stock when they got there, and many times it wasn't. So they'd be offered some other kind of contraceptive. They might be offered condoms, for example, which clinics tended to have in good supply because of the AIDS epidemic. But condoms are often unhelpful for women trying to avoid pregnancy. Women have told me over and over again, "If I ask my husband to wear a condom, he will beat me up. It's like I'm accusing him of being unfaithful and getting HIV, or I'm saying that I was unfaithful and got HIV." So condoms were useless for many women, and yet health clinics would claim they were stocked up on contraceptives when all they had was condoms.

After I heard most of the women tell the same story about walking a long way and not getting the shot, I stepped inside the room and found that, in fact, the clinic did *not* have the shot everyone had come for. That wasn't a minor inconvenience for these women. It wasn't just a matter of driving to the next pharmacy. There was no pharmacy. And they had come miles on foot. And there were no other contraceptives these women could use. I have no idea how many of the women I met that day became pregnant because the health center was out of stock.

An unplanned pregnancy can be devastating for women who can't afford to feed the children they already have, or who are too old, too young, or too ill to bear children. My visit with Meena opened my eyes to women who didn't know about contraceptives. My visit to Malawi opened my eyes to women who knew about contraceptives and wanted contraceptives but couldn't get them.

It hadn't come as a revelation to me that women want contraceptives. I knew it from my own life, and it was one of the things we supported at the foundation. But after these trips, I began to see it as central, as the first priority for women.

When women can time and space their births, maternal mortality drops, newborn and child mortality drops, the mother and baby are healthier, the parents have more time and energy to care for each child, and families can put more resources toward the nutrition and education of each one. There was no intervention more powerful—and no intervention that had become more neglected.

In 1994, the International Conference on Population and Development in Cairo drew more than 10,000 participants from around the world. It was the largest conference of its kind ever held and a historic early statement on the rights of women and girls. It urged the empowerment of women, set goals for women's health and education, and declared that access to reproductive health services, including family planning, is a basic human right. But funding for family planning had dropped significantly since Cairo.

That's a big reason why contraceptives were the number one issue on my mind in 2010 and 2011. And the subject kept coming up everywhere I went. Back in Seattle, in October 2011, Andrew Mitchell, the UK's secretary of state for international development, was attending a malaria summit hosted by our foundation and approached me with an idea: Would we be interested in hosting another summit the following year, this one on family planning? (This, of course, became the summit I described in chapter 1.)

The idea of an international family planning summit struck me as both scary and exciting, a huge project. I knew that we would have to emphasize setting goals, improving data, and being more strategic. But I also knew that if we were going to set ambitious goals and reach them, we had to meet a much tougher challenge. We had to change the conversation around family planning. It had become impossible to have a sensible, rational, practical conversation about contraceptives because of the tortured history of birth control. Advocates for family planning had to make it clear that we were not talking about population control. We were not talking about coercion. The summit agenda was not about abortion. It was about meeting the contraceptive needs of women and allowing *them* to choose for themselves whether and when to have children. We had to change the conversation to include the women I was meeting. We needed to bring in *their* voices—the voices that had been left out.

That's why, just before the summit, I visited Niger, a patriarchal society with one of the highest poverty rates in the world, an extremely low use of contraceptives, an average of more than seven children per woman, marriage laws that allow men to take several wives, and inheritance laws that give half as much to daughters as to sons and nothing to widows who don't have children. Niger was, according to Save the Children, "the worst place in the world to be a mother." I went there to listen to the women and meet those mothers.

I traveled to a small village about an hour and a half northwest of the capital and met with a mother and okra farmer named Sadi Seyni. (I mentioned her in chapter 1, too.) Sadi was married at 19—old for Niger, where 76 percent of all girls are married by 18.

After her first child, Sadi was pregnant again in seven months. She didn't learn about family planning until after she had her third child and a doctor at her local one-room clinic told her about contraceptives. She then began spacing her births. When I met her, Sadi was 36 years old and had six children.

We talked in Sadi's home. She sat opposite me on her bed with two children beside her, another snuggling into her lap, another standing behind her on the bed, and two older children sitting nearby. They were all dressed in colorful fabrics, each a different pattern, and Sadi and the older girls wore headscarves; Sadi's was a solid purple. The sun was pouring in through the windows, only partially blocked by a sheet they'd put up, and Sadi answered my questions with an energy that showed she was glad to be asked.

"When you don't do family planning," she said, "everybody in the family suffers. I'd have a baby on my back and another in my belly. My husband had to take on debt to cover the basics, but even that wasn't enough. It's complete suffering when you don't do family planning, and I have lived that."

I asked her if she wanted another child, and she said, "I don't plan on having another child until the little one is at least four. If she's four, she can play with her little brother or sister; she can take him on her back. But now, if I were to bring her a little brother, it would be like punishing her."

When I asked her how women find out about contraceptives, she said, "The good thing about being a woman here is that we gather a lot and talk. We talk when we meet under a tree to pound our millet. We talk at feasts after a baby is born, and that is where I talk to others about getting a shot and how much easier it is to use than the pill. I tell them you should take it to give yourself and your children a break."

What mother wouldn't understand that—giving yourself and your children a break?

The following day I visited the National Center for Reproductive Health in Niamey, the capital. After our tour, five women who were there to get services joined us for conversation. Two young women told us about their lives, and then we heard from an outspoken 42-year-old mother named Adissa. Adissa had been married off at age 14, gave birth to ten children, and lost four. After her tenth pregnancy, she visited the family planning center to get an IUD and has not been pregnant since. That's caused her husband and sister-in-law to look on her with suspicion and ask why she hasn't delivered recently. "I'm tired," she told them.

When I asked Adissa why she decided to get an IUD, she sat and thought for a moment. "When I had two kids, I could eat," she said. "Now, I cannot." She receives from her husband the equivalent of a little over a dollar a day to take care of the entire family.

I asked Adissa if she had any advice for the younger women who were there, and she said, "When you can't take care of your children, you're just training them to steal."

A few minutes later we all got up to leave. Adissa walked toward the tray of food that no one had touched, put most of it in her bag, wiped a tear from her eye, and left the room.

As I took in everything I had just heard, I wanted so badly for everyone to hear Adissa. I wanted a conversation led by the women who'd been left out—women who want contraceptives and need them and whose families are suffering because they can't get them.

## The Old Conversation—That Left Women Out

Changing the conversation has been a lot harder than I expected because it's a very old conversation, grounded in biases that don't easily go away. The conversation has been in part a response to the work of Margaret Sanger, who has a complex legacy.

In 1916, Sanger opened the first clinic in the United States that offered contraceptives. Ten days later, she was arrested. She posted bail, went back to work, and was arrested again. It was illegal to distribute contraceptives. It was also illegal to prescribe them, to advertise them, or to talk about them.

Sanger was born in 1879 to a mother who would eventually have eighteen pregnancies and care for eleven children before dying of tuberculosis and cervical cancer at the age of 50. Her death encouraged Sanger to become a nurse and work in New York City slums with poor immigrant mothers who had no contraceptives.

In a story she told in her speeches, Sanger was once called to the apartment of a 28-year-old woman who was so desperate to avoid another baby that she had performed a self-induced abortion and nearly died. The woman, realizing how close she'd come to killing herself, asked the doctor how she could prevent another pregnancy. The doctor suggested she tell her husband to sleep on the roof.

Three months later, the woman was pregnant again, and after another attempt at abortion, Sanger was again called to the apartment. This time the woman died just after Sanger arrived. As she told it, that prompted Sanger to quit nursing, swearing that she would "never take another case until I had made it possible for working women in America to have the knowledge to control birth."

Sanger believed women could achieve social change only if they were able to prevent unwanted pregnancy. She also saw family planning as a free speech issue. She gave public talks. She lobbied politicians. She published columns, pamphlets, and a newspaper about contraceptives—all illegal at the time.

Her arrest in 1916 made her famous, and over the next two decades more than a million women wrote to her in desperation, pleading for help in getting contraceptives. One woman wrote, "I would do anything for my two children to help them go through a decent life. I am constantly living in fear of becoming pregnant again so soon. Mother gave birth to twelve children."

Another wrote, "I have heart trouble and I would like to be here and raise these four than have more and maybe die."

A southern farm woman wrote, "I have to carry my babies to the field, and I have seen their little faces blistered by the hot sun. . . . Husband said he intended making our girls plow, and I don't want more children to be slaves."

These women's letters were published in a book called *Motherhood in Bondage*. Sanger wrote, "They have unburdened their souls to me, a stranger, because in their intuitive faith, they are confident that I might extend help denied them by husbands, priests, physicians, or their neighbors."

When I read some of these letters, a song came into my head that often comes when I'm engaged in my work—a song I heard constantly in church as a child, attending Mass five times a week at Catholic school. It's heartbreakingly sad, beautiful and haunting, and its refrain goes, "The Lord hears the cry of the poor." The nuns taught us that it was the role of the faithful to respond to that cry.

The cries for help in these women's letters are hard to distinguish from the voices of Meena or Sadi or Adissa or many other women I've talked to in health clinics and in their homes. They are far apart in time and place, but alike in their struggle to be heard and in the reluctance of their communities to listen.

Across cultures, the opposition to contraceptives shares an underlying hostility to women. The judge who convicted Margaret Sanger said that women did not have "the right to copulate with a feeling of security that there will be no resulting conception."

Really? Why?

That judge, who sentenced Sanger to thirty days in a workhouse, was expressing the widespread view that a woman's sexual activity was immoral if it was separated from her function of bearing children. If a woman acquired contraceptives to *avoid* bearing children, that was illegal in the United States, thanks to the work of Anthony Comstock.

Comstock, who was born in Connecticut and served for the Union in the Civil War, was the creator, in 1873, of the New York Society for the Suppression of Vice and pushed for the laws, later named for him, that made it illegal—among other things—to send information or advertisements on contraceptives, or contraceptives themselves, through the mail. The Comstock Laws also established the new position of Special Agent of the Post Office, who was authorized to carry handcuffs and a gun and arrest violators of the law—a position created for Comstock, who relished his role. He rented a post office box and sent phony appeals to people he suspected. When he got an answer, he would descend on the sender and make an arrest. Some women caught in his trap committed suicide, preferring death to the shame of a public trial.

Comstock was a creation of his times and his views were amplified by people in power. The member of Congress who introduced the legislation said during the congressional debate, "The good men of this country . . . will act with determined energy to protect what they hold most precious in life—the holiness and purity of their firesides."

The bill passed easily, and state legislatures passed their own versions, which were often more stringent. In New York, it was illegal to talk about contraceptives, even for doctors. Of course, no women voted for this legislation, and no women voted for the men who voted for it. Women's suffrage was decades away. The decision to outlaw contraceptives was made for women by men.

Comstock was open about his motives. He said he was on a personal crusade against "lust—the boon companion of all other crimes." After he attended a White House reception and saw women in makeup, with powdered hair and "low dresses," he called them "altogether most extremely disgusting to every lover of pure, noble, modest woman." "How can we respect them?" he wrote. "They disgrace our land."

In Comstock's eyes, and the eyes of his allies, women were entitled to very few roles in life: to marry and serve a man, and bear and take care of his children. Any detour from these duties brought disrepute—because a woman was not a human being entitled to act in the world for her own sake, not for educational advancement or professional accomplishment, and certainly not for her own pleasure. A woman's pleasure, especially her sexual pleasure, was terrifying to the keepers of the social order. If women were free to pursue their own pleasure, it would strike at the core of the unspoken male code, "You exist for *my* pleasure!" And men felt they needed to control the source of their pleasure. So Comstock and others did their best to weaponize stigma and use it to keep women stuck where they were, their value derived only from their service to men and children.

The need of men to regulate women's sexual behavior persisted in the US even after the Second Circuit court in 1936 ruled that physicians could advise their patients on birth control methods and prescribe contraceptives. In spite of this advance, many restrictions on contraceptives stayed in place nationally, and in 1965, when the Supreme Court ruled in *Griswold v. Connecticut* that contraceptive restrictions were an intrusion into marital privacy, *the Court lifted restrictions for married people only*! It didn't mention the rights of the unmarried, so single women were still denied contraceptives in many states. This is not so long ago. Women in their seventies still come up to me at events and tell me, "I had to trick my doctor into thinking I was married or I couldn't get contraceptives." Unmarried women weren't given the legal right to contraceptives until *Eisenstadt v. Baird* in 1972.

This strand of the conversation on family planning is grounded in society's discomfort with women's sexuality, and this line of conversation absolutely endures today. If a woman speaks up in public for the value of contraceptives in a health plan, some misogynistic male voices will try to shame her, saying, "I'm not going to subsidize some woman's sex life."

Shaming women for their sexuality is a standard tactic for drowning out the voices of women who want to decide whether and when to have children. But that is not the only discussion that has diminished the voices of women. Many interests have tried to control women's births in ways that make it hard to have a focused conversation on contraceptives today.

In an effort to control their populations, both China and India adopted family planning programs in the 1970s. China created a one-child policy, and India turned to policies that included sterilization. In the 1960s and '70s, population control was embraced in US foreign policy based on predictions that overpopulation would lead to mass famine and starvation and possibly to large-scale migration because of a lack of food.

Earlier in the twentieth century, birth control advocates in the United States had also pressed their case, many of them hoping to help the poor avoid having unwanted children. Some of these advocates were eugenicists who wanted to eliminate "the unfit" and urged certain groups to have fewer children, or none at all.

Sanger herself supported some eugenicist positions. Eugenics is morally nauseating, as well as discredited by science. Yet this history is being used to confuse the conversation on contraceptives today. Opponents of contraception try to discredit modern contraceptives by bringing up the history of eugenics, arguing that because contraceptives have been used for certain immoral purposes, they should not be used for *any* purpose, even allowing a mother to wait before having another child.

There is another issue that has blocked a clear and focused conversation on contraceptives, and that issue is abortion. In the United States and around the world, the emotional and personal debate about abortion can obscure the facts about the life-saving power of contraception.

Contraceptives save the lives of mothers and newborns. Contraceptives also reduce abortion. As a result of contraceptive use, there were 26 million fewer unsafe abortions in the world's poorest countries in just one year, according to the most recent data.

Instead of acknowledging the role of contraceptives in reducing abortion, some opponents of contraception conflate it with abortion. The simple appeal of letting women choose whether or when to have children is so threatening that opponents strain to make it about something else. And trying to make the contraceptive debate about abortion is very effective in sabotaging the conversation. The abortion debate is so hot that people on different sides of the issue often won't talk to each other about women's health. You can't have a conversation if people won't talk to you.

The Catholic Church's powerful opposition to contraceptives has also affected the conversation on family planning. Outside of governments, the Church is the largest provider of education and medical services in the world, and this gives it great presence and impact in the lives of the poor. That is helpful in so many ways, but not when the Church discourages women from getting the contraceptives they need to move their families out of poverty.

Those are some of the conversations that have been heard in the world over the previous hundred years or more. Each conversation helped drown out the voices and the needs of women, girls, and mothers. And that gave us a crucial purpose for holding the first summit in 2012: to create a new conversation led by the women who'd been left out—women who wanted to make their own decisions about having children without the interference of policy-makers, planners, or theologians whose views would force women to have more, or fewer, children than they wanted.

I gave the opening address that day in London and asked the delegates: "Are we making it easier for women to get access to the contraceptives they need when they need them?" I talked about the trip I had made a few years before to the poor Nairobi neighborhood of Korogocho, which means "shoulder to shoulder." I was discussing contraceptives there with a group of women, and one young mother named Marianne said, "Do you want to know why I use contraceptives?" Then she held up her baby and said, "Because I want to bring *every good thing* to this child before I have another." That desire is universal, but access to family planning is not. I reminded everyone at the conference that this was why we were all here.

Then, to make the point that the summit was all about having women own the conversation, I stepped aside and invited another woman to come to the stage and complete my talk.

The speaker was Jane Otai, who had served as my translator when I spoke to Marianne. After growing up in Korogocho in a family of seven children, Jane had left to earn a university degree, and then returned to help girls who faced the same challenges she had.

Jane talked to the conference about growing up poor and said, "My mother told me, 'You can become what you want to become. All you have to do is study very hard—and wait. Don't have children as early as I did.'" Jane closed by saying, "Because someone told me about family planning very early, I was able to space my children and delay my first pregnancy. That is why I am here. If not for family planning, I would be like any other child in Korogocho."

## After the Summit—a Bit of the Old Conversation

The summit was hailed as a success, with unprecedented pledges of financial support and partnership from organizations and governments around the globe, but I learned pretty quickly that changing the conversation would still be difficult.

Immediately after the summit, I was singled out for criticism in a front-page story in *L'Osservatore Romano,* the official Vatican newspaper. I had "gone astray," it said, and was "confused by misinformation." It went on to say that every foundation is free to donate to whatever cause it wants, but not "to persist in disinformation and present things in a false way." The article charged that I was dismissing or distorting the value of natural family planning, and suggested that I was being manipulated by corporations who stood to gain from selling contraceptives. The movement we had launched at the summit to expand access to contraceptives was based on "an unfounded and second-rate understanding," it said. I did notice that the article focused on me, and corporations, and Church teaching, but not the needs of women.

*Forbes* later said the story showed that I "could take a punch." I expected the punch—I also expected the online comments that referred to me as "former Catholic Melinda Gates" or "so-called Catholic Melinda Gates"—but it stung anyway. My first reaction was "I can't *believe* they would say that!" (That's probably a typical response for a beginner in public life!) After a couple of days, though, I had calmed down, and I got why the Church said what it said. I didn't agree, but I understood.

I have met with high-ranking officials of the Church since the conference, but our meetings didn't focus on doctrine or differences. We talked about what we could do together for the poor. They know that I understand the basis of the Church's opposition to contraceptives, even though I don't agree. They also know we share some similar concerns. We are both opposed to any effort to coerce women to limit the size of their families, and we are both opposed to wealthy countries imposing their cultural preference for small families on traditional societies. If a woman does not want to use contraceptives because of her faith or values, I respect that. I have no interest in telling women what size families to have, and no desire to stigmatize large families. Our work in family planning leaves the initiative to the women we serve. That's why I believe in voluntary family planning and support a wide range of methods, including natural fertility awareness methods for any woman who prefers them.

Obviously, though, I've felt the need to express my differences with the Church. Contraceptives save the lives of millions of women and children. That's a medical fact. And that's why I believe all women everywhere, and of any faith, should have information on the healthy timing and spacing of pregnancies, and access to contraceptives if they want them.

But there is a big difference between believing in family planning and taking a lead advocacy role for a cause that goes against a teaching of my church. That is not something I was eager to do. When I was trying to decide if I should go ahead, I talked it over with my parents, with priests and nuns I've known since childhood, with some Catholic scholars, and with Bill and the kids. One of my questions was "Can you take actions in conflict with a teaching of the Church and still be part of the Church?" That depends, I was told, on whether you are true to your conscience, and whether your conscience is informed by the Church.

In my case, the teachings of the Catholic Church helped form my conscience and led me into this work in the first place. Faith in action to me means going to the margins of society, seeking out those who are isolated, and bringing them back in. I was putting my faith into action when I went into the field and met the women who asked me about contraceptives.

So, yes, there is a Church teaching against contraceptives—but there is another Church teaching, which is love of neighbor. When a woman who wants her children to thrive asks me for contraceptives, her plea puts these two Church teachings into conflict, and my conscience tells me to support the woman's desire to keep her children alive. To me, that aligns with Christ's teaching to love my neighbor.

Over the past decade or so, I've tried to get inside the mind of some of the Church's most committed opponents of contraceptives, and I have wished they could see inside mine. I believe that if they faced an appeal from a 37-year-old mother with six children who didn't have the health to bear and care for another child, they would find a way in their hearts to make an exception. That's what listening does. It opens you up. It draws out your love—and love is more urgent than doctrine.

So I don't see my actions as putting me at odds with the Church; I feel I am following the higher teaching of the Church. I have felt strong support in this from priests, nuns, and laypeople who've told me that I am on solid moral ground when I speak up for women in the developing world who need contraceptives to save their children's lives. I welcome their guidance, and it's reassuring to me that a huge majority of Catholic women use contraceptives and believe it's morally acceptable to do so. I also know that ultimately moral questions are personal questions. Majorities don't matter on issues of conscience. No matter what views others may have, I am the one who has to answer for my actions, and this is my answer.

## The New Conversation—Under Way in Nairobi

As I mentioned before, as we began planning the summit we were determined that it be focused on goals and strategy, and we ended the summit determined to make contraceptives available to 120 million more women in the sixty-nine poorest countries in the world by 2020, on the way to universal access by 2030. Those were the goals. Four years later, at the midpoint of our campaign, our data showed there were 30 million additional users of contraceptives; that meant that 300 million women overall were using modern contraceptives. The round number sounded nice, but it was 19 million below what we'd hoped.

We had learned two important lessons by 2016. First, we needed better data. It was crucial to help us predict demand, see what was successful, and help pharmaceutical companies design products that have fewer side effects and are easier to use and cheaper to buy.

Second, we learned again that women do not make decisions in a vacuum; they are hemmed in by the views of their husbands and mothers-in-law—and those traditions do not change easily. So along with gathering more data, we had to learn more about how our partners work in communities that might be hostile to contraceptives, and how they address the sensitive question of making contraceptives available to unmarried youth.

To understand some of the biggest successes in these areas, I traveled to East Africa in the summer of 2016. Kenya was well ahead of its goals, and I wanted to see why.

On my first stop, in Nairobi, I went to visit the women who gather the data. We call them resident enumerators, or REs for short. They go door-to-door in their communities, interviewing women and entering the data into their cell phones. They are trained to ask very personal questions: "When is the last time you had sexual intercourse? Do you use contraceptives? What kind? How many times have you given birth?" Most of the time, the women they interview are eager to answer. There's something empowering about being asked. It sends a message that *your life matters*.

The resident enumerators learn a lot about the lives of the

respondents that they don't really know how to turn into data. One RE told me she went to a house where a woman lived with her husband and twelve children. The woman's husband was opposed to family planning and turned the RE away at the door. But the mother ran into the RE later—REs live in the communities they serve—and asked her to come talk to her nine daughters when her husband wasn't around. Unfortunately, we don't yet know how to make the data capture the story of the controlling husband who sent the RE away.

I saw this data challenge myself when I went to a local household with Christine, one of the REs. When she was halfway done with her survey, she handed me a mobile phone and told me to finish up. I asked the mother how many children she had, and she said two daughters. When I asked how many times she had given birth, she said three—and started to cry. She told me about her son, who died the day he was born, and then told me a painful story of her husband turning violent, beating her, and destroying all the chairs and supplies in the hair salon she had built. She took her daughter and moved in with her mother. Then she had a second daughter with another man, but she never made a reliable income, so she had trouble paying school fees and medical expenses for her daughters, and sometimes couldn't afford to feed them.

I was listening to this heartbreaking story, trying to enter the information in the phone, and I became frustrated that her story overwhelmed the system set up to capture the facts of her life. How did her abusive marriage affect her income? How did her income affect her use of contraceptives and the health of her children? Even if I had asked the questions, I had no place to put the answers.

What would it take to get a more complete picture of her life? You can't meet a need you don't know about. I brought this question up later when I talked to the women who had gone door-to-door with me. They all nodded their heads. Every one of them had more questions they wanted to ask—about clean water, children's health, education, domestic violence. Christine said to me, "If we could ask about domestic violence, we would be signaling to the woman that this is unacceptable behavior." She's exactly right, and this is an ongoing project of ours—improving data systems so we can ask more questions, gather more information, and capture the texture of women's stories. There will never be a system that captures everything, so there will never be a substitute for hearing women's stories. But we have to keep working to get better data so we can understand the lives of the people we serve.

## Let's Plan

I was also eager to visit Kenya to see a program called Tupange, a slang term for "Let's plan." Tupange had done a terrific job boosting contraceptive use in three of Kenya's largest cities, and I could see why. My hosts took me to a community outreach event that had the feel of a fairground. Tupange representatives sang and danced outside to help attract foot traffic to the fair, and inside, volunteers walked around wearing giant aprons festooned with contraceptives—the most effective methods hanging at the top, the least effective methods on the bottom. There were stands offering counseling on HIV, HPV, family planning, and nutrition. It was a great way to make healthcare and family planning easy to get and stigma-free. There was a striking openness in the atmosphere and conversations—an amazing accomplishment when promoting a subject that is still in many ways taboo. Tupange has many initiatives, but each of them, in one way or another, challenges stigma and social norms. That is the key to their success.

One of the first Tupange leaders I talked to was Rose Misati, who as a little kid was filled with dread every time her mom became pregnant. Each new baby meant more childcare duties for Rose, more chores in the home, and less time to study. She began staying home from school and falling behind her classmates. When Rose was 10, just after her mom had given birth to her eighth child, a healthcare worker came to the house, and every day after, Rose remembers her mom asking her to bring her a glass of water and one of her pills. There were no more little brothers and sisters for Rose to take care of.

Sometimes the best thing a mother can do for her children is not have another child.

Rose got back up to speed at school, did well on her exams, and gained entrance to the University of Nairobi. She is now a pharmacist, and she says she owes it to her mom's family planning. So when the Tupange program asked her to help, she jumped at the chance, and became a big voice for sending community health workers door-to-door. "I know this works," she said. "This is how they found my mom."

Rose knocks down stigma by the way she talks about contraceptives. When she opens meetings, she says her name, her title, and the method of family planning she uses. Then she asks others to do the same. The first time she tried it, people were shocked. Now

people embrace it, and the stigma is weakening. I've come to learn
that stigma is always an effort to suppress someone's voice. It forces
people to hide in shame. The best way to fight back is to speak up—
to say openly the very thing that others stigmatize. It's a direct attack on the self-censorship that stigma needs to survive.

Rose weakens another stigma by reaching out to men to talk
about "a women's issue." "When you get men on board," she says,
"their wives' use of contraceptives is nearly universal." She tells
the men family planning will make their children healthier, stronger, and more intelligent—and because fathers see intelligent
children as proof of their own intelligence, they're open to this
argument.

Male allies are essential. It's especially beneficial to have male
allies who are religious leaders, like pastor David Opoti Inzofu.
David grew up in Western Kenya with conservative parents who
didn't use family planning or discuss it. As a young man, he thought
family planning was a population control conspiracy. But he started
listening after he met Tupange workers who said that timing and
spacing pregnancies could improve the health of the mother and child
and allow families to have only as many children as they could take
care of. That convinced him. Not only do he and his wife use contraceptives, but he uses his pulpit to share the message with his congregation. He points to the Bible verse 1 Timothy 5:8: "And whoever
does not provide for relatives and especially family members has
denied the faith and is worse than an unbeliever."

I was thrilled to see Tupange giving so much attention to the
role men play in family planning. Men shouldn't want to have more
children than they can care for. They shouldn't oppose women's

desire to space the births of their children. Men's and women's interests should be aligned, and the men who see this are the ones we want leading family planning discussions with other men.

I met another male ally who became an advocate after an unplanned pregnancy nearly ruined his life. Shawn Wambua was only 20 years old when Damaris, his girlfriend, got pregnant. His church was on the verge of excommunicating him, his girlfriend's family was furious with him, and he had no one to turn to—both his parents had died.

Shawn visited a health center and learned about contraceptives. Then he asked Damaris to marry him, and she got an IUD to delay the next child until they were sure they could provide for two. Shawn then became connected with Tupange and created a group called Ndugus for Dadas ("brothers for sisters"). Every week, he leads a group of about twenty young men who talk about contraceptives and other issues they're facing. Shawn is also taking his advocacy to the church that nearly threw him out. When church leaders spoke out against a reproductive health bill, saying that sex education would encourage promiscuity, he publicly challenged them. He believes the church is wrong to think that young people aren't having sex or that contraceptives will give young people ideas they didn't have before. "We share the same room with our parents," he said. "We know what they are doing."

Remarkably, the church elders now allow Shawn to talk to young members of the congregation about reproductive health, as long as it's not on church grounds. This, I think, is a perfect metaphor for the split convictions that the keepers of the old order often have. They know there is a truth on the other side that they're not acknowledging, and while they can't bring themselves to express that truth personally, they realize they can allow the message to be spread by others. It's a special experience to see when that happens, and to meet the people whose stories are so compelling that they lead the elders to soften their views.

When social norms help everyone prosper, they have natural support because they're in people's self-interest. But when norms protect the power of certain groups or forbid or deny things that are a natural part of human experience, the norms can't stand on their own; they have to be enforced by some sanction or stigma.

Stigma is one of the biggest barriers to women's health, and people in Tupange figured out that sometimes the best way to weaken a stigma is to defy it openly. This can be a risky strategy when the time isn't ripe. But Tupange workers knew the culture, and they knew that their courage and defiance would force a public discussion that would expose the flaws and unfairness of the stigma. As more people challenged the stigma, there was a shift, the stigma softened, and the culture changed. This can work whether the stigma is a social norm or a national law.

## When Stigma Is Law

Tupange shows the power of group action, but it takes individuals to bring a group into being.

Pia Cayetano is one of those individuals. When she was elected to the Philippine Senate in 2004, there was no national law guaranteeing access to contraceptives. Local jurisdictions could do anything they wanted. Some required a prescription to get a condom. Some required pharmacies to keep a record of every contraceptive purchase. Others banned contraceptives outright. Legislators had drafted a bill to legalize contraceptives across the country, but the Catholic Church was opposed, and the bill sat idle for more than a decade.

As a result, the maternal death rate was rising in the Philippines—even as it declined around the world. By 2012, fifteen Filipino women were dying every day in childbirth. Unlike most of her colleagues, Pia knew the wonders and dangers of childbirth. When she was pregnant with her son, Gabriel, she learned from an ultrasound that he had chromosomal abnormalities. She carried Gabriel to term and cared for him for nine months until he died in her arms. Her loss allowed her to hear with special compassion the stories of Filipino women who couldn't get contraceptives. There was Maria, who suffered from hypertension, had three unplanned pregnancies in a row, and died during the third. There was Lourdes, who was unable to care for her eight children and had three of them taken away and given to others to raise.

When a sympathetic president, Benigno Aquino III, took office in 2010, Pia decided to push for the bill in the Senate, highlighting the tragedy of maternal death and saying, "No woman should die giving life." She was told it was hopeless, that her colleagues would amend the bill till she didn't recognize it, and she'd never get the votes to pass it anyway. Other senators heaped doubt on her statistics about mothers dying and downplayed the significance of the mothers' deaths, saying that more men die at work, so women shouldn't complain. Not one of her male colleagues would support her until one senator stood with her—her younger brother, Alan Cayetano.

When Alan joined the debate on the side of his sister, men began to acknowledge the hardship the current law created for the poor. As the bill gained momentum, the Catholic bishops intensified their opposition, and Pia and other supporters were targeted in personal ways.

One Catholic congregation hung a banner outside its church with the names of the legislators who voted for the reproductive health bill. The banner was headlined TEAM DEATH. In sermons, priests would mention Pia's name on the list of people going to hell. She stopped taking her family to Mass so her children wouldn't have to hear it.

At the same time, Pia told me, some Catholic leaders reached out to her, offering political guidance and building a bridge of quiet cooperation around common goals of supporting the poor and reducing the deaths of mothers and infants. With a lot of effort and delicate diplomacy, the bill passed—and was immediately challenged in court.

A year later, in May of 2013, I met Pia at the Women Deliver conference in Malaysia. She told me she had to put off a long-planned visit to the United States so she could be in the Philippines to make oral arguments at the Supreme Court. The following spring I saw Pia's name in my inbox with a joyous message and a link to this news article:

*MANILA, Philippines (UPDATED)—After earning the ire and ridicule of some male colleagues for defending the controversial reproductive health law, a beaming Senator Pia Cayetano hailed the Supreme Court decision upholding the legality of its key provisions.*

*"This is the first time I can honestly say I love my job!" she said.*

*"Many women who have questioned this, even men, are people who have access [to reproductive health], so this is for the poor, especially poor women, who do not have the ability to access their own information and services."*

It's easy for me to connect very deeply with people doing this work, and I've always found it exciting to watch and applaud the success of people I admire, even when I have to do it from a distance. But I especially appreciate the chance to show my love and respect in person. When Pia came to the US for a conference in Seattle in 2014, I was able to give her a big hug, and it reminded me how much all of us in this work need one another. We give energy to one another. We lift each other up.

## The United States

The work of Pia and others in the Philippines was a huge success. In another success, Great Britain has cut its teen pregnancy rate—once the highest in Western Europe—in half over the last two decades. The experts say success came from connecting young people to high-quality, nonjudgmental counseling.

The United States has also been successful in bringing down teen pregnancy rates. The country is at a historic low for teen pregnancy and a thirty-year low for unintended pregnancy. Progress is due largely to expanded use of contraceptives, which accelerated thanks to two initiatives begun in the prior administration—first, the Teen Pregnancy Prevention Program, which spends $100 million a year to reach low-income teens in communities across the United States; and second, the birth control benefit in the Affordable Care Act, which allows women to get contraceptives without paying for them out of pocket.

Unfortunately, that progress is in jeopardy—both the drop in unwanted pregnancies and the policies that helped make it happen. The current administration is working to dismantle programs that provide family planning and reproductive health services.

In 2018, the administration put out new guidelines for Title X, the national family planning program, which serves 4 million low-income women a year. The guidelines basically state which kinds of programs the government will fund, and this version does not mention any of the modern contraceptive methods approved by the Food and Drug Administration. Instead, it named only natural family planning, or the rhythm method, even though *less than 1 percent* of the low-income women who rely on this federal program use that method.

The administration also proposed eliminating the Teen Pregnancy Prevention Program, which would end a crucial supply of contraceptives for teens who need them. We're talking about young people living in poor areas who have few options, like teens from the Choctaw Nation in Oklahoma and teens in foster care in Texas. In place of these services, the administration wants to offer abstinence-only programs.

Overall, its goal seems to be replacing programs proven to work with programs proven *not* to work, which, in effect, means that poor women in the US will have less access to effective contraceptives, and many poor women will have more children than they want to just because they're poor.

Another dire threat to family planning in the United States comes in a policy the current administration has proposed but not yet finalized—one that would stop federal funds from going to healthcare providers that perform, or even refer for, abortions. This is similar to laws already enacted in Texas and Iowa, where the effect on women has been devastating. If this policy takes effect nationally, more than a million low-income women who now rely on Title X funding to get contraceptive services or cancer screenings or annual exams from Planned Parenthood will lose their healthcare provider. A half million women or more could be left with no provider at all; there are simply not enough community health clinics to serve the women who will be cut off by this policy. If you're a woman with no economic means, you may have nowhere to go.

For women outside the United States, the administration has proposed cutting its contribution for international family planning in half and cutting its contributions to the UN Population Fund to zero—even though there are still more than 200 million women in the developing world who want contraceptives but can't get them. Congress has so far stood up for poor women and largely maintained previous levels of international family planning funding. But the world needs the US administration to be a leader for women's rights, not an opponent of them.

The administration's new policies are not trying to help women meet their needs. There isn't any reliable research that says women benefit when they have children they don't feel ready to raise. The evidence says the opposite. When women can decide whether and when to have children, it saves lives, promotes health, expands education, and creates prosperity—no matter what country in the world you're talking about.

The US is doing the opposite of what the Philippines and the UK did. It is using policy to *shrink* the conversation, suppress voices, and allow the powerful to impose their will on the poor.

Most of the work I do lifts me up, some of it breaks my heart, but this just makes me angry. These policies pick on poor women. Mothers struggling in poverty need the time, money, and energy to take care of each child. They need to be able to delay their pregnancies, time and space their births, and earn an income as they raise their children. Each one of these steps is advanced by contraceptives, and each one is jeopardized by these policies.

Women who are well off won't be harmed, and women with a stable income have options. But poor women are trapped. They will suffer the most from these changes and can do the least to stop them. When politicians target people who can't fight back, that's bullying.

It's especially galling that some of the people who want to cut funding for contraceptives cite morality. In my view, there is no morality without empathy, and there is certainly no empathy in this policy. Morality is loving your neighbor as yourself, which comes from *seeing* your neighbor as yourself, which means trying to ease your neighbor's burdens—not add to them.

The people who push these policies often try to use the Church's teaching on family planning for moral cover, but they have none of the Church's compassion or commitment to the poor. Instead, many push to block access to contraceptives *and* cut funds for the poor. They bring to mind the words of Christ in the Gospel of Luke: "And you experts in the law, woe to you, because you load people down with burdens they can hardly carry, and you yourselves will not lift one finger to help them."

It's the mark of a backward society—or a society moving backward—when decisions are made for women by men. That's what's happening right now in the US. These are not policies that would be in place if women were making decisions for themselves. That's why it's heartening to see the surge of women activists across the country who are spending their time knocking on doors, supporting family planning, and changing their lives by running for office.

Perhaps a big push for women's rights has been triggered by these recent efforts to take rights away. I hope that's what's happening now, and that the fire that drives this defense of family planning fuels a campaign to advance *all* rights of women, all around the world—so that in the future, in country after country, more and more women will be in the room, sitting at the table, leading the conversation when the policies that affect our lives are made.

# CHAPTER FOUR

# Lifting Their Eyes

## *Girls in Schools*

When Meena asked me to take her children home with me, I realized we had to do more than help mothers give birth safely. We had to see the big picture. That's why we expanded our foundation's work in family planning. But every time I've thought, *Okay,* now *we're seeing the big picture,* I'd meet another woman or girl who would show me a *bigger* picture. And my most important teachers were not the experts we would meet with in Seattle. They were women and girls who met us in their towns and talked about their dreams.

One of our teachers was Sona, a 10-year-old girl from Kanpur who lived in a very poor village, home to one of the lowest castes in India. The people there lived in about six feet of trash because of the work they did. They would go gather the garbage from other areas, bring it to their village, pick out whatever had value, and sell it—leaving what ever they couldn't sell strewn on the ground around them. That's how they earned a living.

Gary Darmstadt, my foundation colleague, met Sona on a visit he made to Kanpur in 2011 to talk about family planning. On the morning of his visit, he greeted our partners from the Urban Health Initiative, and they all walked through the village till they came to a place where meetings were held. As soon as the group stopped, a cluster of women gathered around them, and Sona—the only girl among them—walked up to Gary and handed him a toy parrot. She had found the raw material in the trash, bent and carved it into the form of a bird, and now offered it as a gift. When Gary thanked her, Sona looked him in the eyes and said, "I want a teacher."

Gary was a bit thrown by this. He had come that day to discuss family planning with the women of the village, not to start a school. For the moment he left aside Sona's comment and began talking with the mothers. It turned out they were very happy with the program. For the first time, they felt they were beginning to gain some control over their lives. It's always gratifying to hear good news. But throughout the conversation, Gary could see Sona standing around waiting, and as soon as there was a pause, she would say to Gary, "I want a teacher. You can help me." Over the course of three hours, probably fifty times she looked at Gary and said, "I want a teacher."

After the group had finished its talk, Gary paused and asked one of the mothers about Sona. The woman said, "You know, we've told you how family planning has helped us. It's had a tremendous impact on our lives. But the truth is, unless our kids get an education they're going to be right back here living in trash like us. It's good to be able to control the size of my family, but I'm still poor, and I'm still picking trash. Our kids are going to have the same life unless they can go to school."

It takes courage to ask for what you want—especially when it's more than people think you should have. Sona had a magical combination of courage and self-regard that allowed her to ask for a teacher even though she was a low-caste girl whose parents picked trash for a living. She probably didn't even know how bold she was being. But the women around her knew it—and they didn't tell her to be quiet, which in a way made Sona the spokeswoman for the group, saying what the mothers believed but didn't quite have the nerve to say.

Sona had no leverage over anyone. She had only the innocence of a child speaking her truth and the moral power of a girl saying "Please help me grow." That power guided her in the right direction, because more than almost anything else society and government provide, education determines who thrives.

Education is a vital step on the path to empowerment for women—a path that starts with good health, nutrition, and family planning and prepares you to earn an income, run a business, form an organization, and lead. In this chapter, I want to introduce you to some heroes of mine, people who have opened up opportunities for students who were treated like outsiders undeserving of an education.

But first, let me tell you what happened to Sona. Our partners who met with Gary to talk about family planning knew the area and its laws well. When they heard Sona saying "I want a teacher" and listened to a mother talking to Gary about education, they got together and developed a plan. The land Sona lived on with her family was not registered with the government. In fact, they had no legal right to be there. So our partners went to the local government and did all the work needed to get Sona and her neighbors registered as inhabitants, which was an amazing thing; the government officials could have found all kinds of tricks to block the change, but instead they supported it. When the people were declared legal inhabitants of that land, the families were then entitled to a full range of government services—including schools. Sure enough, Sona got a teacher. She got books. She got a uniform. She got an education. And not just Sona, but every kid in the village, and it was all triggered by one small child with courage looking a visitor in the eyes, offering him a gift, and saying over and over again, "I want a teacher."

### The Incomparable Lift of School

The lift that comes from sending girls like Sona to school is stunning—for the girls, their families, and their communities. When you send a girl to school, the good deed never dies. It goes on for generations advancing every public good, from health to economic gain to gender equity and national prosperity. Here are just a few of the things we know from the research.

Sending girls to school leads to greater literacy, higher wages, faster income growth, and more productive farming. It reduces premarital sex, lowers the chance of early marriage, delays first births, and helps mothers plan how many children to have and when. Mothers who have had an education do a better job learning about nutrition, vaccination, and other behaviors necessary for raising healthy children.

Half of the gains in child survival in the past two decades can be attributed to gains in mothers having gone to school. And mothers who have gone to school are more than twice as likely to send their own children to school.

Girls' education can have transformative effects on the health, empowerment, and economic advancement of women. But we still don't have detailed knowledge about why. What *happens* in the minds and lives of girls that leads to these benefits? Are the changes triggered by literacy, role modeling, the practice of learning, or just getting out of the house?

Many of the principal claims I've heard make strong intuitive sense: Women who can read and write can do better navigating the health system. School helps girls learn how to tell the stories of their families' health issues to health providers. Learning from teachers helps mothers learn how to teach their own children. Also, when girls are in the classroom and see how they can learn, they begin seeing themselves differently, and that gives them a sense of their own power.

This last idea is especially exciting to me—it means that women can use the skills they learn in school to dismantle the rules that keep them down. When I visit schools and talk to students, this is where I feel the power of the work. It goes back to high school for me, when I volunteered in a crowded public school tutoring kids in math and English. When kids learn something new, they see they can grow; that can lift their sense of self and change their future.

People who've been treated like outsiders often come to school thinking that they don't deserve more and should never demand it because they won't get it. Good schools change that view. They instill in their students an audacious sense of who they are and what they can do. These high expectations are in direct conflict with society's low expectations for these kids, and that's the point. Schools that empower students on the margins are subversive organizations. They foster a self-image in the students that is a direct rebuke to the social contempt that tries to keep them in their place.

You can see this socially defiant mission in good schools everywhere—in the United States, South Asia, or sub-Saharan Africa. These schools change the lives of students who've been led to believe that they don't matter, that they don't deserve a full chance.

## Schools That Lift Up Their Students

About ten years ago on a trip to Los Angeles, I was talking with nearly a hundred African American and Latino kids from tough backgrounds when one young woman asked me: "Do you ever feel like we're just somebody else's kids whose parents shirked their responsibilities, that we're all just leftovers?"

That question shocked me. It made me want to embrace her and convince her that her life had infinite value, that she had the same rights and deserved the same opportunities as anyone. But on the same trip, I saw why she didn't think that way. I talked to another young woman who was taking a course of studies that, even if she aced it, would not prepare her for college, or anything else. I looked at her curriculum. One lesson involved reading the back of a can of soup in a grocery store and knowing the contents. That was math class. And that wasn't rare. I've seen the same thing in many school districts across the United States—one group of students studying Algebra II while others were taught how to balance a checkbook. The first group would head to college and careers; the second group would struggle to make a living.

Bill and I focus most of our US philanthropy on education. We believe a strong system of schools and colleges is the best idea our country has ever had for promoting equal opportunity. We focus on increasing the number of black, Latino, and low-income students who earn a high school diploma and also the number who continue their education *after* high school—both boys and girls. (I'm working to expand pathways into technology for girls, and girls of color specifically, through my office, Pivotal Ventures—a company I started to help spark social progress in the US.) The best schools lift up the students who never thought they could rise. And when you see that happen, it can make you cry with joy.

In 2015, Bill and I went to visit Betsy Layne High School in Floyd County, Kentucky, a rural community in the Appalachia region that has been devastated by the decline of the coal industry. *The New York Times* has called this area one of the toughest places in the country to live. Six counties in the region were ranked in the nation's bottom ten in income, educational attainment, unemployment, obesity, disability, and life expectancy. Amazingly, though, over the previous ten years, when the region went into economic decline, student achievement in Floyd County had climbed from 145th in the state to 12th. We wanted to see how they were doing it.

We were joined on our trip by Vicki Phillips, then head of K–12 education at our foundation. Vicki knew about the challenges facing these students and teachers because she had lived them. As Vicki tells it, when she was a little girl, her mom and stepfather got married and paid the $500 owed in back taxes to buy a four-room house with dirt floors and broken windows that sat on a farm her family still owns in rural Kentucky. That's where Vicki grew up, helping her family raise pigs, grow vegetables, and hunt for supper. They had a hand pump in the house and an outhouse in the back, and they didn't think they were poor because none of their neighbors had any more than they did.

Vicki said her teachers were deeply devoted to their students, but looking back, she realized that the education she was getting wasn't preparing her for college; it was preparing her to stay where she was. "Where I grew up," she said, "a lot of people didn't *want* excellence in schools. It scared people.

"My parents expected I would graduate high school, live in the community, get married, and have a family. The day I came home and told my parents, 'I'm going to college,' my stepfather said, 'And you will not be my daughter. And if you do, don't you ever come back. Don't *ever* plan on coming back, because your values are not our values.'"

Vicki and her dad had fights about it till the day she left. He would say, "This is a safe community. You're my daughter. Why would I feel comfortable about you doing that?"

Then, Vicki says, he drilled into the most sensitive issue. "Why do you want to leave home, anyway? Everything you might ever need is here. Is what we have not good enough? Are you saying we're not good enough for you?"

These are common questions for families who fear that going

to college means moving out and never coming back. As they see it, their culture doesn't hold people back; it holds people together. In their eyes, pursuing excellence can look like disowning your people.

That's how it was where she grew up, Vicki said. There was nothing in her culture to propel her to college. She made it there after meeting a girl from the rich end of the county who said to her one day, "What do you *mean*, you're not going to college?!? You're as smart as I am." She began pushing Vicki to take tougher courses, take the college boards, and seek scholarships. That's how Vicki overcame a culture that didn't want her to go to college. She joined her friend's culture. If you want to excel, Vicki says, you have to get support from the people around you. Very few people can do it alone.

Vicki was willing to face the conflict that came from challenging her culture. But she worked it out with her family, even with her dad. A year after she left, she got a call at college. The familiar masculine voice on the other end said, "Vicki, this isn't working. Let me drive down and bring you home for a visit." Her dad picked her up and took her home, and everybody reconnected. She and her dad got close again. They stayed honest about their differences, and he continued to tease her in an affectionate way for the rest of his life, calling her (in their family of staunch Republicans) "our little Democrat."

Vicki went on to become a special education teacher, a school superintendent, and a state secretary of education who worked to change the norms and empower people who'd been pushed out. That's the same drive that we found in the faculty at Betsy Layne.

The personalities there were exuberant and unforgettable—starting with Cassandra Akers, the principal. Cassandra has loved Betsy Layne for a long time; she was valedictorian of the class of 1984. She still lives in the house where she grew up, which her parents sold to her when she started teaching. She's the oldest of seven children and the only member of her family to graduate from college, so she knows the community and the struggle the kids face.

"Our students have to know that we expect great things," she said. "But they also know that whatever they need, we're going to help them get it, whether it's teaching, tutoring, extra help, food, clothes, a bed, whatever. You have to take care of all of them."

One of the biggest challenges in changing the culture is lifting up the self-image of the kids. They've had self-doubt planted in their minds by society, the media, even members of their own families. Mothers and fathers who've never achieved their goals can easily plant their own doubts in the minds of their kids. When those doubts get into kids' heads, they're hard to change. People who are the victims of doubt often feel targeted, and the psychologist at Betsy Layne told me that many students felt that the world not only didn't care about them but was rooting against them.

The harder people's challenges have been, the more important it is to surround them with a new culture and a fresh set of expectations. One of the math teachers I met, Christina Crase, told me that she tells the students on the first day of school, "Give me two weeks!" She doesn't want to hear about their failures, or how much they hate math, or how far behind they are. She says, "Give me a chance to show you what you can do!"

One of her projects is to help the kids build small-scale Ferris wheels. The first time she presented the idea to her class, the students thought she was nuts, but they were happy to do it. It was easier than learning math! So they poured themselves into their projects and built their Ferris wheels, and by the time Ms. Crase was explaining sine and cosine functions, all she had to do was link the idea back to the Ferris wheel, and they all got it.

The kids held this material so firmly in their minds that a few of them came running into class after visiting a local carnival and said, "Ms. Crase, we didn't ride the Ferris wheel."

"Why not?" she asked.

"We didn't trust its structural integrity," they said. Then they began explaining in the language of calculus and trigonometry.

After visiting classrooms, Bill and I joined some students for lunchtime pizza in the cafeteria. A number of them admitted they'd been afraid to take AP classes because "APs are for the smart kids." But they took AP courses anyway and learned a lot, and the most important thing they learned was "We *are* the smart kids."

Great schools don't just teach you; they change you.

## Girls in Schools

Equal education moves people toward empowerment, but unequal education does the reverse. Of all the divisive tools that are used to push people to the margins, unequal education is the most damaging and enduring. Unless there is an explicit effort to include everyone, schools will never be a remedy for exclusion; they will be a cause of it.

Yet in spite of the astounding benefits that come when girls get an education, more than 130 million girls around the world are still not in school. This number is often cited as progress—but only because the barriers to girls going to school used to be worse. During my own school years, far more of the world's boys went to school than girls. This disparity was common in countries that didn't require kids to go to school.

In past decades, though, governments have made a major push to reverse that, and they've been largely successful. Most countries are enrolling equal numbers of boys and girls in primary school. But the goal, of course, is not to make sure girls are deprived of an education at the same rate as boys. The goal is to remove all the barriers that keep children from attending school, and in some places the barriers are still more significant for girls than for boys. This is particularly true in secondary school, generally considered to be school years seven through twelve. In Guinea, just one in four girls is enrolled in secondary school, while almost 40 percent of boys are. In Chad, fewer than a third of girls are enrolled in secondary school, but more than two out of three boys are. In Afghanistan, too, just over a third of girls are enrolled in secondary school, compared to nearly 70 percent of boys. These barriers continue in university. In low-income countries, for every hundred boys who continue their education after high school, only fifty-five girls do the same.

Why are there fewer girls than boys in secondary and postsecondary school? Economically, sending girls to school is a long-term investment, and for families in extreme poverty, the focus is on survival. Families can't spare the labor, or they can't come up with the school fees. Socially, women and girls don't need an education to play the roles that traditional societies have prepared for them. In fact, women getting an education threatens traditional roles. Politically, it's instructive to see that the most extremist forces in the world, like Boko Haram, which kidnapped 276 schoolgirls in northeast Nigeria in 2014, have been especially hostile to girls' education. (Boko Haram's name actually means "Western education is forbidden.") The extremists are saying to women, "You don't have to go to school to be who we want you to be." So they burn down schools and kidnap girls, hoping that families will keep their girls home out of fear. Sending girls to school is a direct attack on their view that a woman's duty is to serve a man. One young woman who challenged that view is Malala Yousafzai, the Pakistani woman who was shot by the Taliban in 2012 when she was 15 years old. Malala was known in the world before then. She was inspired by her father, who ran a chain of schools, to write a blog talking about her life as a girl going to school under the Taliban. Her blog was widely read, and Archbishop Desmond Tutu nominated her for the International Children's Peace Prize.

So when Malala was shot, it was not a random shooting of a girl who was going to school; it was a targeted hit on a well-known activist by people who wanted to silence her and frighten others who shared her views. But Malala wouldn't keep quiet. Nine months after she was shot, she spoke at the United Nations. "Let's pick up our books and our pens," she said. "They are our most powerful weapons. One child, one teacher, one book, and one pen can change the world."

A year later, in 2014, Malala became the youngest person ever to win a Nobel Peace Prize. (She learned she'd won the award when she was sitting in chemistry class!)

I had met Malala after she won the prize, and like everyone else, I was inspired by her story. But when I hosted her at an event in New York in 2017, I was even more inspired by how she *told* her story. Malala didn't focus on herself. She said, "I believe we can see *every girl in school* in my lifetime, because I believe in local leaders." Then she told us how she was supporting activists who were getting girls into school all around the world—and, in a surprise, she invited those activists present to come forward. They came to the stage and Malala turned the microphone over to the people who inspired her.

Today, Malala's foundation is investing in activist-educators all over the world. One activist is educating teachers in Brazil about gender equality. Another is campaigning to end school fees in Nigeria. Another, in Malala's home country of Pakistan, is hosting forums to persuade parents to send their daughters to school.

I'm going to follow Malala's example. I'm going to tell you about some of the people and organizations who've inspired me. Governments from Kenya to Bangladesh have put massive financial resources behind making school free for girls. The UN and the World Bank have major girls' education programs. And there are organizations, such as the Campaign for Female Education, that are making school possible for the poorest girls. Among all the great programs, I want to focus on three that especially impress me: one from a national government, one from a global organization, and one from a young Maasai woman who stood up and changed centuries of tradition.

## "Agents of Development"

One of the most inspiring ideas on girls' education comes from Mexico. Some of the best ideas in development are simple ideas—*after* you've heard them. But it takes a visionary to dream them up and make them work. In Mexico in the 1990s, many families still couldn't send their kids to school because they needed the children's labor to get by. So in 1997, a man named José Gómez de León and his colleagues put forward a new idea. They believed that women and girls were "agents of development," and they put that belief into practice.

The government would treat education as if it were a job and pay families to send their kids to school. Payments would be based on what children could earn if they were working for pay—a third-grader might earn $10 a month, a high schooler $60. They called the program Oportunidades—"opportunities."

They made sure the payments for the children were given directly to the mothers. And because girls were more likely than boys to drop out, girls got a bit more money than boys to stay in school.

After the program was phased in, girls who were in Oportunidades had a 20 percent greater chance of being in school than girls who weren't. Not only did more girls go to school, but those who did stayed in school longer. The program helped nearly 6 million families.

Just twenty years after the program began, Mexico has achieved gender parity in education—not only at the primary school level but also in high school and college. And Mexico has the world's highest percentage of computer science degrees awarded to women.

The World Bank called Mexico's effort a model for the world and said it was the first to focus on extremely poor households. Fifty-two countries now have some form of the same program.

## Breakthrough in Bangladesh

I had been aware of the work of the Bangladesh Rural Advancement Committee since it won a Gates Global Health Award in 2004, and I visited the founder, Fazle Hasan Abed, in Bangladesh in 2005. In addition to its visionary work in health and microcredit, BRAC is the largest secular private educator in the world, and focuses on educating girls.

Back in the 1970s, when Bangladesh was recovering from its liberation war, most families were running small farms, struggling to get by and relying heavily on their children, especially their daughters. As a result, by the 1980s, less than 2 percent of Bangladeshi girls were in school by the fifth grade, and half as many girls as boys were in high school. That was when Fazle Hasan Abed, a Bangladeshi who'd become a successful businessman in Europe, decided to come home to found BRAC and start building schools.

When BRAC got started in 1985, every one of their schools had to have at least 70 percent girls. All of the teachers had to be female, and they all had to come from the community, so that parents wouldn't be afraid for their daughters' safety. Each BRAC school set its own schedule to accommodate the growing season, so that families who relied on girls' farm labor could send their daughters to school. Also, BRAC schools provided books and materials free of charge, so that costs could never be an excuse for keeping a girl out of school.

As the number of BRAC schools grew, the country's religious extremists—recognizing that schools lift women up—began to burn the schools down. Abed rebuilt them. He said BRAC's goal was to challenge the culture that kept women down, and the arsonists proved that BRAC was getting results. Today, Bangladesh has more girls attending high school than boys, and BRAC runs 48,000 schools and learning centers around the world. It goes to the most dangerous places in the world for a girl to attend school and slowly helps those cultures change.

## Challenging Centuries of Tradition

In many rural areas of sub-Saharan Africa, young girls are expected to obey the customs of their culture, not challenge them, and certainly not change them.

Kakenya Ntaiya, like most other 13-year-old girls in Kenya's Maasai community, had her future mapped out for her the second she was born. She would go to primary school until she reached puberty. Then she would submit to female genital cutting and drop out of school and be married to the boy she became engaged to at age 5. From that day on, she would fetch water, gather wood, clean house, cook food, and work the farm. It was all planned out, and when the life of a girl is planned out, the plan serves everyone but the girl.

Change starts when someone says "No!"

I first learned about this courageous Maasai girl when our foundation helped fund a film contest for documentaries about people changing the world, and the winner was a film featuring Kakenya.

Kakenya wanted to be a teacher. That meant she couldn't quit her studies when she hit puberty. She couldn't get married and cook and clean for her new family. She had to stay in school. I can't imagine her boldness. I was a good kid in grade school. I wanted everyone's approval. I was lucky that what I wanted for my life was in line with what my parents and teachers wanted, but if my dreams and theirs had diverged, I don't know if I could have stood up for myself.

Kakenya apparently didn't have those doubts. When she turned 13, she offered her father a deal: She would submit to the female genital cutting, but only if he would agree that she could stay single and keep going to school. Kakenya's father knew that if she didn't go through with the cutting, he would be shamed in the community. He knew his daughter was tough enough to defy tradition. He took the deal.

On the designated day, Kakenya walked into a cow pen near her home and, as her entire community watched, a local grandmother cut off her clitoris with a rusty knife. She bled profusely and fainted from the pain. Three weeks later, she was back in school, determined to become a teacher. By the time she graduated, she'd won a full scholarship to attend college in the United States.

Unfortunately, the scholarship did not include plane fare, and the people in her village weren't likely to pay her way. When she told people she got a scholarship and asked for their help, they said, "What a lost opportunity. It should've been given to a boy."

Kakenya had the courage to defy tradition, but she also had the wisdom to make it work in her favor. In the Maasai community, there is a belief that good news comes in the morning. So every morning, Kakenya would knock on the door of one of the influential men in the village. She promised that if they helped her get her education, she would come back and make a difference.

Eventually, she got the village to buy her a plane ticket.

In the US, she not only got her undergraduate degree but earned a PhD in education. She worked for the UN. She learned about the rights of women and girls. Most important, she says, "I learned that I did not have to trade part of my body to get an education. I had a right."

When she returned home to her village to keep her promise, she asked the elders to help her build a school for girls. "Why not a boys' school?" they asked. One of the elders said he saw no need for girls to get educated, but he did respect that she'd come back home to support the village. "We have several sons who have gone to the United States for school," he said. "Kakenya is the only person that I can think of that has come back to help."

Kakenya saw the opening. If the boys don't come back to help and the girl does, she told him, it makes more sense to educate the girls. Now, the elder says, "What she tells us, it touches us. . . . She brought a school and a light and is trying to change old customs to help girls get a better life."

The elders donated the land for the new school, and in 2009 the doors opened at the Kakenya Center for Excellence. The school reaches girls in the late primary school years, when they're likely to be pulled from school to be married, and helps them make the transition to secondary school. The Kakenya Center provides uniforms, books, and tutoring. In return, parents must agree that their daughters won't undergo female genital cutting and won't be married off while they're still in school. Some of the center's students have scored in the top 2 percent of the Kenya National Examinations and have gone to college in Kenya and abroad.

I don't have any idea how people find the guts to speak up against waves of tradition, but when they do, they always end up with followers who have the same conviction but not quite the same courage. That's how leaders are born. They say what others want to say, and the others then join them. That's how a young woman can change not only her life but her culture.

## Changing How a Girl Sees Herself

All the women I've talked to and all the data I've seen convince me that the most transforming force of education for women and girls is changing the self-image of the girl who goes to school. That's where the lift is. If her self-image doesn't change, then going to school will not change the culture, because she will be using her skills to serve the social norms that keep her down.

That is the secret of an empowering education: A girl learns she is not who she's been told she is. She is the equal of anyone, and she has rights she needs to assert and defend. This is how the great movements of social change get traction: when outsiders reject the low self-image society has imposed on them and begin to author a self-image of their own.

Sister Sudha Varghese understands this better than anyone else

I know. When Sudha was a young girl attending Catholic school in southwestern India, she read an article about nuns and priests who worked with the poor and knew instantly she'd been called to a life of service. She joined a religious order, became a nun, and began her work. But it didn't inspire her. The motherhouse was too comfortable. The people she served weren't poor enough. "I wanted to be with the poor," she said, "and not just the poor but the very poorest among them. So I went to the Musahar."

Her faith taught Sudha to go to the people on the margins. She chose the people on the outermost margins. Musahar means "rat eaters." They are "untouchables" in India—people born into a caste system that sees them as less than human. They can't enter village temples or use the village path. They can't eat at the same tables or use the same utensils as others. The Musahar are considered so low that they are looked down on by other "untouchables."

When Sudha first decided she wanted to work with the Musahar, there was no organized way to do it, nothing set up for her to join. So she traveled alone to a Musahar community in northeast India and asked the people there for a place to stay. She was given space in a grain shed and immediately began working to improve the lives of the lowest of the Musahar—the women and girls.

Sudha told me that she had once asked a group of Musahar women to raise their hands if they had never been struck by their husbands. Not a single woman raised her hand. She thought the question had been misunderstood, so she asked the group, "Raise your hand if your husband has struck you." Every woman raised her hand. Every woman there had been beaten in her own home.

Outside the home was worse. Musahar women live under

constant threat of sexual violence and face a continuous stream of scorn. If the girls walk outside the village, people will hiss *"Musahar"* at them and remind them they are untouchable. If they laugh or walk too freely, someone will grab them by the arm and tell them their behavior is unacceptable for a Musahar girl.

From the time they are born, society is constantly telling them they are completely worthless.

After working for more than twenty years to improve the lives of Musahar women—facing scorn because she lived with "untouchables" and receiving death threats for her efforts to bring rape cases to trial—Sudha decided in 2005 that the best thing she could do was to open a free boarding school for Musahar girls.

Sister says, "All they have known and heard and seen is 'You are like dirt.' They have internalized this. 'This is my lot. This is where I belong. I don't belong on the chair. I will sit on the floor, and then no one can tell me to go any lower than that.' All their lives they are told, 'You are the last. You are the least. You do not deserve to have.' They learn very fast to keep quiet, not to expect changes, and don't ask for more." The goal of Sister's school was to turn that self-image around.

One of my favorite lines of scripture is "The last will be first, and the first will be last." That, to me, captures Sister Sudha's mission, and she starts by teaching her students that no matter what their society tells them, they should never put themselves last.

She called her new school Prerna, which means "inspiration" in Hindi. When I visited Sister there, she took me by the hand and introduced me to all the students we met, by name. The girls are often homesick when they arrive, and Sister stopped to comfort a young girl who was in tears, stroking her head as they spoke. Sister touched all the girls as she talked to them, putting her hand on a shoulder, patting another on the back, pouring out love to everyone she saw. If the girls get hurt, she bandages them herself—because they aren't used to having anyone care that they are wounded. Sister wants to undercut their sense that they are untouchable.

She says, "When they get here, they are just looking at the ground all the time. To get their eyes lifted is something." The girls I met held their heads high and looked me in the eye. They were respectful, curious, bright-eyed, confident—even a bit cheeky. One girl heard I was married to Bill Gates and asked me how much money I had on me. I turned my empty pockets inside out as Sister and I laughed.

The girls at Prerna all take the usual subjects like English and math and music and computers. But Sister also offers a special curriculum, something she'd been trying to teach the Musahar from the moment she arrived. She insists that every girl know her rights—the right to study, the right to play, the right to walk around freely, the right to be safe, the right to speak up for herself.

They've been told their whole lives that they are the lowest of the low, but here they are taught "You have the same rights as other people. And you must use your skills to defend your rights."

Defending yourself is not just an abstract lesson. Sister Sudha makes the girls learn karate. They're often targets of sexual violence at home or in the field, so Sister wants them to know that they have the right not to be attacked—and they have the power to take on their attacker. (It turns out that teaching physical defense skills is proven to reduce violence against adolescent girls.) Sister told me with pleasure the story of one of her girls delivering a kick to the gut of a drunken man interested in sexual favors. He stumbled off and never came back.

Learning karate—or any form of self-defense—was bewildering to girls who'd been trained to accept abuse. But the girls worked hard, and their progress was so impressive that their karate teacher suggested that Prerna send a team to India's national karate competition. Sister agreed; she thought it would be a good experience for them to travel. The girls won gold and silver medals in nearly every event they entered. The chief minister of Bihar asked to meet them and offered to pay their way to the world championships in Japan. *The last will be first.*

Sister got them passports and tickets and travel documents. This seemed like a good opportunity to see the world. The girls came home with seven trophies—and something more: a sense of what it's like to be in a culture that doesn't look down on them.

"They were so astonished by how much respect people showed them," Sister said. "They said, 'Imagine, bowing to me, speaking to me this way.'"

It was the first time these girls had ever been in a society that didn't scorn them. It helped them see that in their own country they were treated with low regard not because of a flaw in them, but because of a defect in society.

A low self-image and oppressive social customs are inner and outer versions of the same force. But the link between the two gives outsiders the key to change. If a girl can lift up her view of herself, she can start to change the culture that keeps her down. But this isn't something most girls can do on their own. They need support.

The first defense against a culture that hates you is a person who loves you.

Love is the most powerful and underused force for change in the world. You don't hear about it in policy discussions or political debates. But Mother Teresa, Albert Schweitzer, Mohandas Gandhi, Dorothy Day, Desmond Tutu, and Martin Luther King Jr. all did hardheaded, tough-minded work for social justice, and they all put the emphasis on love.

It's a mark of our culture's uneasiness with love that political candidates never talk about it as a qualification for holding public office. In my view, love is one of the highest qualifications one can have. As one of my favorite spiritual teachers, Franciscan priest Richard Rohr, says, "Only love can safely handle power."

For me, love is the effort to help others flourish—and it often begins with lifting up a person's self-image.

I've seen the power of self-image in my colleagues and my classmates, in grade schools and universities, and in the world's greatest companies. I've also seen it in myself. When I was in high school in Dallas, I met with a college guidance counselor I knew who wanted to offer me some advice. After I told her about the schools I was hoping I might attend, she told me I couldn't get into any of them and should scale back my ambitions. She said I should focus on going somewhere closer to home.

If I had not been surrounded by people who lifted me up, I might have taken her advice and sold myself short. Instead I stormed out of that talk furious with her and twice as determined to reach my goals. That wasn't *my* power; it was the power of the people who had shown me my gifts and wanted me to flourish. That's why I am so passionate about teachers who can embrace girls and lift them up—they change the course of their students' lives.

A girl who is given love and support can start to break the self-image that keeps her down. As she gains self-confidence, she sees she can learn. As she learns, she sees her own gifts. As she develops her gifts, she sees her own power; she can defend her own rights. That is what happens when you offer girls love, not hate. You lift their gaze. They gain their voice.

# CHAPTER FIVE

# The Silent Inequality

*Unpaid Work*

Four or five years ago, before I had begun to focus on the household burdens of the world's poorest women, I heard the story of Champa.

Champa was a 22-year-old mother from a tribal area in central India, living in a two-room hut with her husband, her in-laws, and her three children. Ashok Alexander, the first head of our India office, paid her a visit one morning with a group of health workers. They had been told that Champa had a 2-year-old girl named Rani who was suffering from severe acute malnutrition, a condition that leads quickly to death if it's not treated.

As the guests arrived, Champa came out of her home with her child in one arm and a pallu covering her face—a form of dress worn by the most conservative Hindu women to limit their contact with men. Champa was carrying a clutch of medical papers she couldn't read. She pushed them into Ashok's hands.

As Ashok took the papers, he looked at Rani. The girl was so malnourished her legs were like sticks, and there was nothing her mother could do about it. Rani could no longer be fed normal food. She required special treatment—a nutrient-heavy diet taken carefully in small doses that could not be given in village conditions. Rani's only hope was to get to the district Malnutrition Treatment Center; if she made it there, she could be back to health within a few weeks. But the center was two hours away by bus, Rani and Champa would have to stay there for two weeks, and Champa's father-in-law had said, "She can't go. She has to stay and cook for the family."

Champa explained all this to the women health workers there as she kept her face covered, even from the other women. She had offered her father-in-law no resistance, even to save the life of her child.

Ashok asked to see the father-in-law. They found him lying down in a field, drunk on homemade rotgut. Ashok said, "Your granddaughter will die if we don't get her treatment."

"She can't go," the father-in-law said. "It's out of the question, leaving for two weeks." When Ashok said again that Rani would die, the man said, "If God takes away one child, he always gives another one. God is very great and generous in this respect."

No one had offered to step into Champa's role and cook. She had no support, no family member willing or able to step in and take on these duties—even in a life-threatening emergency.

Rani's life was saved because the health workers there intervened, taking her to the treatment center with them while Champa stayed home to cook. Rani was lucky. There are many others like her whose mothers are so chained down by household duties and social norms that they don't have the power to protect their children.

Ashok told us later, "This was not an exceptional case. I've seen it time and again. The women have no rights, no empowerment. All they do is cook and clean and let their kids die in their arms, and not even show their face."

## The Unequal Balance of Unpaid Work

For women who spend all their hours doing unpaid work, the chores of the day kill the dreams of a lifetime. What do I mean by unpaid work? It's work performed in the home, like childcare or other forms of caregiving, cooking, cleaning, shopping, and errands, done by a family member who's not being paid. In many countries, when communities don't have electricity or running water, unpaid work is also the time and labor women and girls spend collecting water and gathering wood.

This is reality for millions of women, especially in poorer countries, where women do a much higher share of the unpaid work that makes a household run.

On average, women around the world spend more than twice as many hours as men on unpaid work, but the range of the disparity is wide. In India, women spend 6 hours *a day* doing unpaid work, while men spend less than 1. In the US, women average more than 4 hours of unpaid work every day; men average just 2.5. In Norway, women spend 3.5 hours a day on unpaid work, while men spend about 3. There is no country where the gap is zero. This means that, on average, women do seven years more of unpaid work than men over their lifetimes. That's about the time it takes to complete a bachelor's *and* a master's degree.

When women can reduce the time they spend on unpaid work, they increase the time they spend on paid work. In fact, cutting women's unpaid work from five hours a day to three boosts women's participation in the labor force by about 20 percent.

That is hugely significant because it is *paid work* that elevates women toward equality with men and gives them power and independence. That's why the gender imbalance in unpaid work is so significant: The unpaid work a woman does in the home is a barrier to the activities that can advance her—getting more education, earning outside income, meeting with other women, becoming politically active. Unequal unpaid work blocks a woman's path to empowerment.

Of course, there are some categories of unpaid work that can make life deeply meaningful, including caring for family members. But it's saying nothing against the meaning and value of caregiving to say that it helps all family members—those giving care and those taken care of—when these duties are shared.

In January of 2014, I went with my daughter Jenn to do a homestay with a family in Tanzania—in Mbuyuni, a village just east of Arusha, near Mt. Kilimanjaro.

It was the first overnight visit I did where I stayed with a family in their home, and I was hoping to gain an understanding of people's lives that wasn't available in the books and reports I read, or even in the frank conversations I had with women I met when I traveled.

I was thrilled to be doing this homestay with Jenn, who was 17 years old and in her last year of high school. From the time my children were very young, I've wanted to expose them to the world—not just so they would give back to the people they meet, but so they would *connect* with them. If there is any meaning in life greater than connecting with other human beings, I haven't found it.

I've since also done a homestay with my son, Rory, in Malawi, where a loving couple, Chrissy and Gawanani, and their children took us in for several days. Gawanani taught Rory how to pluck a rooster for dinner. Then he showed Rory the livestock and said, "That pig right there represents my son's education." Rory saw that the way people save for their kids' education differs across cultures, but the drive to help your child flourish is the same.

Phoebe, our youngest, has volunteered in schools and hospitals in East Africa and has her eye on a future that might have her spending a lot of time living in Africa. I hope the exposure to other people and places shapes what the kids do, but even more I want it to shape who they are. I want them to see that in the universal human desire to be happy, to develop our gifts, to contribute to others, to love and be loved—we're all the same. Nobody is any better than anybody else, and no one's happiness or human dignity matters more than anyone else's.

That's a lesson that rang out during Jenn's and my Tanzanian stay with Anna and Sanare, a Maasai couple who lived in a small family compound they had built over the years. They put us up in what had originally been a goat hut. Anna and Sanare had taken over the goat hut when they were married. Later, they built a larger home and moved to another room, and the goats reclaimed their space. But when Jenn and I moved in, the goats moved out for a few days (at least when we kept the door closed!). I learned more during that homestay than I had learned on any previous foundation trip. I especially learned about the burdens a woman carries to make the home and farm run.

Sanare went off in the morning and worked their family's small commercial stall, an hour's walk away along a main road. He usually went there on foot, though sometimes he got a motorcycle ride from his neighbor. Anna stayed home and worked the house and farm, and Jenn and I were able to help her with the household chores and activities.

I'd been traveling to poor communities since we started our foundation, and I was never surprised to see women doing all the cooking, cleaning, and caregiving. But I had never felt the full weight of their days—what they were doing from the moment they woke before dawn to the hour they went to bed long after dark.

Jenn and I went with Anna to chop firewood, using dull machetes on gnarly wood stalks. We walked thirty minutes to fetch water and carried it back in buckets on our heads. We used the wood to build the fire and boiled the water to make tea, then started preparing the food—fetching eggs, sorting beans, prepping potatoes—and cooking it over the flame. The whole family ate dinner together, and we joined the women doing the dishes afterward, all together, at ten at night in the dust of the compound's courtyard. Anna was in motion for seventeen hours a day. The number of hours and the intensity of the labor were a revelation to me. I didn't learn about it in a book. I felt it in my body. I could see that Anna and Sanare had a loving relationship and worked hard to make it equal. Still, Anna and the other women in her village were struggling under a massive burden of unpaid labor that was unevenly distributed between men and women. It wasn't just that it affected women's lives; it darkened their futures.

I talked to Anna while we cooked on a fire in her kitchen, and I asked her what she would do if she had more time. She told me she dreamed of starting her own business, raising a new breed of chicken and selling the eggs in Arusha, an hour and a half's drive away. The income would change their lives, but it was just a dream. Anna had no time to run a business; she spent all her time helping her family get through the day.

I also got a chance to talk to Sanare. He told me he and Anna were worried about their daughter, Grace, who had not passed her test to go to a government-funded secondary school. Grace had one more chance to take the test. If she didn't pass it the second time, her only choice would be a private boarding school, which would be very expensive. If Sanare and Anna could not come up with the money, Grace would lose her chance for a better life.

"I'm worried my daughter's life will be like my wife's," he told me. "If Grace doesn't go to school, she'll stay at home and start spending her time with other girls who have not gone to school. The families will start marrying out the girls, and all her hopes for her life will fade away."

It was an especially complicated situation for Sanare and Anna because their son Penda did pass the test to go to a government school, which is not free but is relatively cheap. So his schooling was assured while Grace's was in doubt.

Penda and Grace are twins. They're in the same year in school.

They're both bright. But Grace does more work around the house than Penda does. When Grace is doing chores, Penda has time to study.

One night when Jenn came walking out of our hut wearing her headlamp, Grace ran up to her and asked, "Can I have your headlamp when you leave so I can study at night after my chores are done?"

Grace was a very shy girl, just 13 years old. But she was bold enough to ask Jenn for the headlamp as a gift. That's how much it mattered to her.

There are millions of girls like Grace, and their extra share of unpaid work could make the difference between a bright and flourishing life and a life of cooking and cleaning and never having time to learn and grow.

When I came back from Tanzania, I could see that unpaid work was more than a symptom of gender bias. It was an area where change could promote women's empowerment, and I wanted to know more.

### The Pioneers

For a long time, economists didn't recognize unpaid work as work—nor the bias that declared certain tasks "women's work," nor the bias that undervalued that work, nor the bias that divided that work unequally between men and women. For years, when economists assessed the productivity of a family farm, they measured the hours of those who worked on the farm, but they didn't count the hours of the women whose cooking and cleaning and caregiving allowed the farmworkers to be productive. Even very sophisticated analysts missed this work for years. They either didn't see it at all or they dismissed its importance, reasoning that this is just the way the world works—women have this additional burden, like child-bearing.

The failure of economists to acknowledge unpaid work got even more absurd as more women entered the formal workforce. A woman would put in a full day at work. When she finished her paid work, she'd help the kids with homework, vacuum the living room, do the laundry, cook the dinner, and put the kids to bed—hours and hours of work that were going completely unnoticed and uncounted.

An economist named Marilyn Waring saw the deep bias and began looking for ways to change it. Elected to New Zealand's Parliament in 1975 when she was just 23 years old, she knew what it was like to be a working woman and to be ignored by the men who made the rules. But when she went looking for the research on women's unpaid work, she couldn't find it. She asked a male economist to help her, and he told her: "Oh, Marilyn, there is no definitive work on it. You know enough; you write it."

So Waring traveled around the world studying unpaid work—and she calculated that if you hired workers at the market rate to do all the unpaid work women do, unpaid work would be the biggest sector of the global economy. And yet economists were not counting this as work.

Waring framed it this way: You pay for childcare in the market-place. You pay for gas to run a stove. You pay a factory to make food from grain. You pay for water when it comes through a tap. You pay for a meal served in a restaurant. You pay for clothes washed in a laundry. But if a woman does it all by herself—caring for children, chopping firewood, grinding grain, fetching water, cooking meals, and washing clothes—no one pays her for it. No one even counts it, because it's "housework," and it's "free."

Waring published the book *If Women Counted: A New Feminist Economics* in 1988. As American economist Julie Nelson put it, "Marilyn Waring's work woke people up."

In 1985, the UN had adopted a resolution asking countries to start counting women's unpaid labor by 2000. After Waring published her book, they moved up the deadline to 1995.

In 1991, a female member of the US Congress introduced a bill that would have required the Bureau of Labor Statistics to count housework, childcare, and other unpaid work in its time-use surveys. The bill didn't pass (women made up only 6 percent of Congress at the time). It was reintroduced in 1993 and again in 1995. Each time, it was rejected.

As Waring wrote, "Men won't easily give up a system in which half the world's population works for next to nothing," especially as men recognize that "precisely *because* that half works for so little, it may have no energy left to fight for anything else."

Finally, in 2003, the Bureau of Labor Statistics started conducting a national time-use survey that measured housework and childcare hours. It shows that men have more time for recreational activities like playing games and exercising, while women not only do more unpaid work but do more work altogether.

Acknowledging this problem has led to some efforts to fix it. After Waring published her book, economist Diane Elson came up with a three-part framework to shrink the gap between the time men spend on unpaid work and the time women spend on it. She called it the 3 Rs: recognize, reduce, redistribute.

Elson says we need to start by *recognizing* that unpaid work is being done. That's why we need to get governments to count the hours women spend in unpaid work. Then we can *reduce* the number of hours that unpaid work takes, using technologies like cookstoves or washing machines or improved breast pumps. Finally, we can *redistribute* the work we can't reduce, so that men and women share it more equitably.

Thinking about the concept of unpaid work shapes the way I see what happens in our house. I want to be honest—I've had terrific long-term help in raising our children and managing our household tasks. I don't know all the personal struggles of other couples who have to balance work with the responsibilities of family and home. I can't speak for them, and I would never compare my situation with theirs. But I do know an imbalance in unpaid work when I see it in my own home—and I see it! It's a lot of work raising kids: taking them to school, to the doctor, to sports practice and drama lessons; supervising homework; sharing meals; keeping the family connected to friends at birthday parties, weddings, and graduations. It takes a lot of time. And at different points, I have come to Bill, exhausted, and said "Help!"

When Jenn started kindergarten in the fall of 2001, we found a school that was ideal for her, but it was thirty or forty minutes away and across a bridge, and I knew I would be driving back and forth from home to school twice a day. When I complained to Bill about all the time I would be spending in the car, he said, "I can do some of that." And I said, "Seriously? You'll do that?" "Sure," he said. "It'll give me time to talk with Jenn."

So Bill started driving. He'd leave our house, drop Jenn at school, turn around, drive back past our neighborhood and on to Microsoft. Twice a week he did that. About three weeks in, on my days, I started noticing a lot of dads dropping kids off in the classroom. So I went up to one of the moms and said, "Hey, what's up? There are a lot of dads here." She said, "When we saw Bill driving, we went home and said to our husbands, 'Bill Gates is driving his child to school; you can, too.'"

One night, a few years later, I was once again the last one in the kitchen after dinner, cleaning up for the five of us, and in a fit of personality I declared, "Nobody leaves the kitchen until Mom leaves the kitchen." There's nothing about being a mom that means I have to clean up while others wander off. Bill supported that—even if I did have to allow him his own niche as the guy who wants to wash the dishes because no one else gets it just right.

If I tried to read the minds of my readers here, I would worry that some of you might be thinking, *Oh, no—the privileged lady is tired of being the last one in the kitchen all by herself. But she doesn't have to get up before the sun. Her kids don't have to take the bus. Her childcare support is reliable. She has a partner who is willing to drive the kids and do the dishes.* I know. I know. I'm describing my own scene not because it's a problem but because it's my vantage point on the problem.

Every family has its own way of coping, and all families can use help managing the tasks of raising kids and running the home.

So in the summer of 2018, I met with researchers I'm funding and asked them to go into ten communities across the United States to study how families manage their caregiving responsibilities—what labor-saving devices they use, how they divide the work, how public policy helps them, and how income affects the way they care for family members.

The way the researchers talked about their work was very moving to me. To care is human—and caring for children or aging parents should be an expression of love. It can offer us some of the most meaningful moments of our lives. But if it's assumed that women will do all these tasks, then caring that should be joyful becomes a burden, and work that should be shared becomes isolating. I hope this research will give us a good picture of the trade-offs Americans make. What prompts some people to forgo income to raise kids and run the household? What prompts some to work from home and others to work *outside* the home? And what are the gender biases embedded in these decisions? Exploring these questions could lead to public policy and market-based approaches that help people juggle the duties of caring for a family—so we can all do more of what makes life meaningful.

## Discovering Hidden Bias

We can't solve inequality in unpaid work until we see the gender bias beneath it. Exposing gender bias is a stunning experience for people who suddenly see their own blind spots—it doesn't matter where on earth you live.

A few years ago, I went to rural Malawi and watched as men

and women held a dialogue designed by a local group to expose hidden bias. I remember sitting in a circle of men and women under a big tree next to a farm plot. In front of us, a farmer named Ester held up a big piece of white presentation paper and drew a clock. She asked the male farmers sitting in the circle to walk her through what their day typically looked like. They chatted about how much time they spent working the field, sleeping, eating, and relaxing.

Then Ester did the same thing for the women. Their days were much more crowded. Between fetching firewood and water, cooking, and caring for kids, these women already had a full-time job before they set foot in the fields. That left them with less time to tend to their own plots—even though their families relied on what they produced to survive.

There was a lot of laughter and joking among the men, but some of it came from the awkwardness of what they were discovering: Their wives worked much harder than they did. The men were clearly surprised. They said they'd never really noticed just how busy their wives were.

In another training that I saw the same day, men and women acted out a typical dinnertime meal. In Malawi, men traditionally eat first, apart from the family, and get first pick of the food. Afterward, their wives and children get what's left. So a group of volunteers acted this out for the group—a man scarfing down the food while his wife and children look on hungrily. Another group of volunteers then showed another way: a family talking and eating together at the table, everyone getting their fill.

A third exercise they did, my favorite, was called Person versus Thing. In this one, a wife and husband switch places. She gets to order him around, directing him to do the tasks that are considered her responsibility. He has to try to imagine her burden of work and see what it feels like to be told what to do. People I spoke with in the village who had done this exercise with their spouses months before told me it was a turning point in their marriage.

After the exercises, I asked a group of men who had already completed this training how it had affected them. One man said he used to hide most of the money he made so that his wife wouldn't make him spend it on the family. Another talked about how he used to force his wife to do things that were "women's work." He said, "At first the word 'gender' had no meaning. My wife tried to explain it to me, but I couldn't see how a man could do a woman's job, or a woman could do a man's job."

The gender exercises changed all that. The men talked about how they now share in the household chores, and they and their wives make decisions together. One man told me that he likes how his wife challenges his decisions because "what she says is sensible."

I asked if it was harder for the men to control their finances now that their wives had a say. All of them conceded that it was. But they said it was worth it because, as one of them put it, "now we work at what will help us both."

These gender dialogues in Malawi gave me a thrill because they showed that gender bias could be changed even in very traditional cultures. Gender bias is often unconscious. Let's see what happens when we bring it to light. Let's see the data. Let's count the hours. Let's share the work and build a sense of partnership. Let's see how life improves when we end the false separation of men's work and women's work.

MenCare, a group headed by Gary Barker, urges men around the world to take on caregiving tasks—and has persuasive data on why men should want to do that. Men who share caregiving duties are happier. They have better relationships. They have happier children. When fathers take on at least 40 percent of the childcare responsibilities, they are at lower risk for depression and drug abuse, and their kids have higher test scores, stronger self-esteem, and fewer behavioral problems. And, according to MenCare, stay-at-home dads show the same brain-hormone changes as stay-at-home moms, which suggests that the idea that mothers are biologically more suited to taking care of kids isn't necessarily true.

## Balancing Unpaid Work; Balancing Relationships

It's true that women are natural caregivers and capable homemakers. But so are men. When women take on those duties exclusively, men's abilities are never developed in those roles, and women's abilities are never developed in other roles. When men develop their nurturing side, it doubles the number of capable caregivers. It helps men build strong bonds with their children that bring joy and last a lifetime. And it helps both men and women develop a wider range of their abilities. Even better, the shift improves the relationships between men and women by diminishing male dominance. Anytime you have a category of tasks that's considered "women's work" that men will not share, it reinforces a false hierarchy that prevents men and women from doing productive work together. Breaking that hierarchy actually leads to *men's* empowerment, because it allows men to discover the power of partnership and lets them develop their caring side.

In *Journey of the Heart*, an extraordinary book on relationships, John Welwood points out what he calls "a natural balancing process" between partners. He writes: "Anything that one partner ignores, the other will feel a greater need to emphasize. Whatever quality of being I deny, such as power, softness or playfulness, my partner will find herself feeling an urge to express more strongly."

This dynamic is what allows some partners to ignore things that they actually do care about, because they know their partner will do the work for both of them. A common example might be a partner who likes social engagements but doesn't do anything to plan them because he knows his partner cares more about them and will plan them if he doesn't.

But leaving to your partner something that you *also* care about leads to separation. When one partner leaves the care of the children to the other, or one partner leaves the role of earning income to the other, they are cutting themselves off from their power—or cutting themselves off from their children. Perhaps the biggest cost is that the two are cutting themselves off from each other.

There is a much better approach. Instead of one partner ignoring a need and the other emphasizing it, we share it. We don't insist that the time spent on the work is mathematically equal, but we both acknowledge what the family needs, and we make plans to take care of it. It is no longer "this is my job, that is yours." It becomes ours.

If you rigidly divide the duties, then you're cutting back on what you share, and that can hurt the partnership. Instead, you can push for a flow where you share everything in different degrees. You develop a partnership that is whole and complementary with a natural hierarchy based on talent and experience, where each can teach and learn, lead and follow, and two can become one.

Of course, if you drop the model of "one partner does these duties and the other partner does those duties," you may have to spend more time talking things out, but that is the path of growth. As Welwood says, "It is the heat and friction of two people's differences that propel them to explore new ways of being."

Much of the research that I've studied on unpaid work is centered on households composed of a man and a woman and children. But we can't expect patterns of unpaid work in a male-female household to apply to other family situations as well. We need to be alert to biases and gather more data so we can see what's common to many families, what's distinctive to certain types, and honor the different forms that families take—whether it's families with two moms, or two dads, or single parents who share custody of their children, or couples who don't have children, or households with grandparents and extended families.

## Equal Partnership—the Hidden Theme in Unpaid Work

The gender imbalance in unpaid work is such a compelling subject for me in part because it's a common burden that binds many women together, but also because the causes of the imbalance run so deep that you cannot solve them with a technical fix. You have to renegotiate the relationship. To me, no question is more important than this one: Does your primary relationship have love and respect and reciprocity and a sense of teamwork and belonging and mutual growth? I believe all of us ask ourselves this question in one way or another—because I think it is one of the greatest longings of life.

Years ago, I was talking to my friend Emmy Neilson about life and marriage and some of the difficulties I was facing at home and work. Emmy is one of my closest friends in life. She was married to John Neilson, one of my best friends at Microsoft. She and John were Bill's and my closest couple-friends until John died at age 37 from cancer, and Emmy and I have become even closer since then. I was sharing with her some of the challenges of being married to Bill, like sometimes feeling invisible, even on projects we worked on together. And she said, "Melinda, you married a man with a strong voice."

That was a piercing line for me, and I've been grateful to her ever since because it gave me perspective. I've been trying to find my voice as I've been speaking next to Bill—and that can make it hard to be heard.

It would have been easy for me to let Bill speak for both of us. But if I let him speak for us, then some important things would not be said, and I wouldn't be challenging myself, or him. I wanted to find my voice, and I wanted an equal partnership, and I couldn't get either without the other, so I had to figure out how to get both with a man who was used to being the boss. I obviously wasn't going to be Bill's equal in everything, nor would he be mine, but could I get an equal partnership? And would Bill *want* an equal partnership? What would be in it for him?

These are some of the questions I wrestled with early in our marriage, and I want to share with you some stories and reflections on how Bill and I moved toward an equal partnership—which, ultimately, is the hidden theme in every discussion of unpaid work.

When we first had Jenn, I felt very alone in our marriage. Bill was CEO of Microsoft at the time, probably at the peak of his commitment there. He was beyond busy; everyone wanted him, and I was thinking, *Okay, maybe he wanted to have kids in theory, but not in reality.* We weren't moving forward as a couple to try to figure out what our values were and how we were going to teach those to our kids. So I felt I had to figure out a lot of stuff on my own.

Early on, we had moved into this nice family-sized house that I had picked out after we got engaged. He was fine with it. But a year and a half later we were moving into this enormous house that Bill had begun building when he was a bachelor. I didn't particularly want to move into that house. In fact, I didn't feel like Bill and I were even on the same page of what we wanted, and we had little time to discuss it. So in the middle of all that, I think I had a crisis of self. Who do I want to be in this marriage? And it pushed me to figure out who I was and what I wanted to do. I was no longer the computer science business executive. I was a mom with a small child and a husband who was busy and traveling a lot, and we were moving into a gigantic house, and I was wondering what people would think of me, because that house was not me.

That's where I was when I began the long climb toward an equal partnership. We've come a long way in the twenty or so years since then. We both clearly wanted an equal partnership, and over time we took the steps we needed to get one.

Bill has said often in interviews that he's always had a partner in everything he's ever done. That's true, but he hasn't always had an *equal* partner. He's had to learn how to be an equal, and I've had to learn how to step up and be an equal. We've had to figure out who's good at what and then make sure we each do more of that and not challenge each other too much on the things we're not good at. But we've also had to figure out what we're going to do in areas where we're both sure of ourselves and we have opposing convictions. That's not something we can run away from, because we share every major decision, and if we can't learn to manage the big disagreements through listening and respect, then even the small disagreements will become large.

One of the most helpful steps for us in developing an equal partnership came after our youngest child, Phoebe, was born in 2002. I was working behind the scenes at the foundation and was content with that. Bill was doing less day-to-day foundation work than I was—he was still full-time at Microsoft—but when he was in public, reporters would ask him questions about the foundation, so he became the voice and face of the foundation, and the press began to write and talk about it as "Bill's foundation." That wasn't the truth of it, and it wasn't how we thought about it either, but it was happening because he was speaking publicly about the foundation and I wasn't. So Bill and I discussed it and agreed that I should step up in public as a cofounder and cochair because we wanted people to know that it was both of us setting the strategy and doing the work. That decision put us on the path to equal partnership.

Bill and I faced a second decision very early on that strengthened our partnership and continues to help us today. We had begun to hire staff at the foundation, and some people were saying, "Look, Melinda is spending more time on education and libraries and work in the Pacific Northwest, and Bill is gravitating toward global health, so why don't they split their roles—Bill work on global health, Melinda work on education and the US programs?"

We discussed this option as a couple, and we agreed we didn't want that. In retrospect, it would have been a huge loss if we'd split our roles, because we share everything now. Whatever we learn and read and see, we share with each other. If we had split our roles, we'd be working in separate worlds, and the two would rarely meet. It might have been equal, but it wouldn't have been an equal *partnership*. It would have been more like parallel play: I won't mess with your stuff and you don't mess with mine. This was another decision that supported our move toward an equal partnership.

Maybe the greatest natural support I had for the idea that a marriage can grow and evolve came from my dad, who was a model for me of how a man can nurture his marriage.

When he and my mom were still young parents, my dad got a call from a friend of his who said, "You and Elaine [*my mom!*] have to go to Marriage Encounter for a weekend. Trust me. Just go. We'll take care of the kids." His friend, also Catholic, had just come back from doing a Church-sponsored workshop on communication and marriage, and he was euphoric about it. My dad was persuaded, so he discussed it with my mom, and she happily agreed. *Of course* she agreed. My mom believes in marriage, believes in retreats, and believes in the Church. So naturally she's going to do a retreat on marriage sponsored by the Church. My mom has done more than anyone else in forming and inspiring my spiritual life over many years. She goes to Mass five times a week. She reads, she goes to silent retreats, and she explores spiritual ideas with passion and openness and curiosity and has always encouraged me to do the same. So it wasn't news to me that my mom was eager to do a marriage retreat with my father. The news was that *he* was excited to go on a retreat with *her*. They went off for a weekend and came home even closer, saying it was one of the best things they ever did together. The moral of the story to me was that a man can call another man and share advice about how to improve their marriages—that men can play a role as guardians and supporters of the union.

So I took my vows with the expectation that Bill would play a role in strengthening our marriage, and fortunately for me, he also had a good model for that in his father. Bill's dad has always had a very strong belief in women's equality, which was obvious to anyone who knew him, but we uncovered even more evidence of it a few years ago. Bill Senior was participating in an oral history project, and the historian showed him an academic paper Bill Senior had written right after he returned to college following military service. The paper was dated December 12, 1946, just after Bill Senior's twenty-first birthday, and includes this passage: "The most outstanding idea in Gatesland is the idea of the perfect state in which women will have all equal rights to men. The female would be as common in the professions and business as the male, and the male would accept female entry into these fields as the normal rather than the abnormal event."

That's a look at the views of the man who helped raise my

husband. (I've said with pride in the past few years that I've raised a feminist son; maybe his grandfather had more to do with it.)

Bill also benefited from the presence of strong and active women in his family. He grew up in a family where his mom had a lot of say. Both parents were building his dad's career, but both were also supporting his mom's work in public service. Mary Maxwell Gates served on the Board of Regents of the University of Washington, her alma mater. In fact, while studying there, she met the student who would become her husband. Early on, when they knew each other only slightly, Mary asked Bill to support her for student body secretary, and he said he was backing another candidate! (Eventually, though, he made the right choice.)

As a member of the UW board, Mary led the effort to divest the university's holdings in South Africa. She also served on numerous corporate boards at a time when few women did. She was the first woman to serve on the board of the First Interstate Bank of Washington, and she was the first woman to chair the National United Way's executive committee.

Mary served the United Way for years in various capacities. When Bill was a teenager, Mary was on the allocation committee, and she and Bill would get into long dinner-table discussions on giving strategies. She gave him his first lessons in philanthropy, then persuaded him to launch the first United Way campaign at Microsoft. When Bill and I got married, his mom, who was very ill with cancer at the time, read aloud at my bridal luncheon a letter she had written to me. Her closing line was "From those to whom much is given, much is expected." She had a lot of influence with Bill. And he had enormous admiration for her.

Bill's grandmother, who also helped raise him, went to the University of Washington and played basketball at a time when most women didn't do such things. So Bill comes from a family of strong, smart, and successful women. The impressions you grow up with in your childhood home make an impact.

To me, it says a lot about the values in Bill's childhood home that his parents gave us as a wedding gift a sculpture of two birds looking out intently toward an unknown place with their gaze eerily together. I put the sculpture by our front door because I like it so much. To me it represents the singular focus of a couple looking to the future together.

So I think Bill wanted an equal partnership because that's what he had in his home growing up. There's another reason, too: He is a ravenous learner and loves to be challenged. When two people challenge each other and learn from each other, it has an equalizing effect. I often talk to Bill about my frustrations with the maddening slow motion of change. He's good at seeing events against a large framework and plotting change in the context of history, science, and institutions. And I teach him some lessons on temperament.

Bill was at a Caltech event in 2016 and the moderator asked him, "Is your approach to managing and working with others still evolving?" Bill said, "Well, I hope so. My wife gives me lots of feedback about when I'm too intense. You know, you can be not intense enough or you can be too intense. I rarely make the mistake of not being intense enough. I'm waiting for her to tell me, 'Hey, you were just way too friendly today. Come on. You let those guys get away with murder, they're wasting our money; you should have spoken up.' As I calibrate, maybe I'll find at least one data point in that regime."

A huge part of what made an equal partnership appealing to Bill is that it's a much more fun and challenging way of being in the world. In the end, though, I think Bill was meant for an equal partnership because it aligns with his deepest values. Early in our work together, we realized that there was an underlying ethos to our philanthropy: the premise that all lives have equal value. It animates *everything*. And one of the things that has made this principle real to me—not as an abstract idea but as an honest mark of the way we see the world—has been seeing how the suffering of others can bring Bill to tears.

That soft side of Bill might surprise people, especially those who've seen the competitive, combative Bill. That is real. Bill has those qualities. But he also has the opposite of those qualities. He can be soft, he can be gentle, he can be very tenderhearted.

Great wealth can be very confusing. It can inflate and distort your sense of self—especially if you believe that money measures merit. Yet Bill is one of the most grounded people I know, and it comes from a clear perspective about how he came to be where he is.

Bill worked incredibly hard and took risks and made sacrifices for his success. But he always understood that there is another ingredient in success, and that is luck—absolute and total luck. When were you born? Who were your parents? Where did you grow up? What opportunities were handed to you? None of us earned those things. They were given to us.

The role of luck in his life isn't just something he admits to me in private moments. It's what he told Malcolm Gladwell when Malcolm asked Bill what accounted for his success. Bill said, "I had a better exposure to software development at a young age than I think anyone did in that period of time, and all because of an incredibly lucky series of events."

So Bill has a sense of humility. Not all the time—I can give you counterexamples. But this is the path of his growth. When he reflects on life and connects with his deepest self, he knows he is not special; he knows his *circumstances* were special—and a man who can see that can see through hierarchy, honor equality, and express his tender heart.

If Bill was taken with me because of my enthusiasm for life, software, people, puzzles, and F. Scott Fitzgerald, I was taken with him because I saw the soft, tender man inside, hidden at first but clearly emerging—the man who is outraged that some lives are seen as worth saving and others aren't. You can't dedicate your life to the principle that all lives have equal value if you think you're better than others. Bill, at his core, doesn't think that way at all, and that is one of the qualities I love most in him.

## I Wanted It

All these marks of temperament and background suited Bill for an equal partnership. Even so, I think we wouldn't have moved very far in that direction if I hadn't made it a priority. Sometimes I asked. Sometimes I had to push.

Let me tell you about the moment I knew I really wanted to be equal partners with Bill at the foundation.

In 2006, Warren Buffett announced the largest single gift anyone ever gave anybody for anything. He committed the bulk of his fortune to our foundation, doubling our endowment and opening up new opportunities for us to invest around the world. We were astounded by his generosity and humbled by his trust. Warren was leaving to Bill and me the decisions about how to spend the money. We were both very excited about what could be accomplished with Warren's gift, but I also felt overwhelmed by the responsibility of deciding how we would invest his wealth and get a return in lives saved and improved.

The three of us were planning a press conference at the New York Public Library to announce the gift. At the time, Bill was running Microsoft, Warren was running Berkshire Hathaway, and I was focusing on the foundation, traveling extensively to see our programs but still not doing a lot of public speaking. This would be the first press conference I had ever done on behalf of the foundation, and I prepared for it intensely. I thought a lot about what I wanted to say and what I had learned and seen around the world. I wanted to honor Warren and be prepared to talk wisely about what we could do with his money.

At the press conference, Bill, Warren, and I answered a lot of questions in depth. When reporters asked how we planned to expand our work, I had answers. We wanted to invest in improving agricultural yields, I said. We wanted to invest in microlending and in fighting more infectious diseases. When reporters asked for specifics, I gave them, offering lessons from my travels.

That was a turning point for me. I honestly hadn't realized how passionate I was about the work until I heard myself talking about it in public with Bill and Warren. It seemed obvious to me then that this needed to be an equal partnership. It wasn't just that I needed it and Bill needed it; the *foundation* needed it. And that's when I knew I really wanted it. I never told Warren the effect his gift had on me, but I should have, long ago. He is an incomparable mentor of mine, and his gift sparked a dramatic upturn in my growth.

That press conference had a similar effect on Bill. It made it clear to him, too, that we needed to be equal partners, and that meant I should be making more public speeches. Of course, that also meant that I would have to rely on Bill for guidance, because he had so much more experience as a public figure. He could have been patronizing about that, but he never was; he was always support-ive. Frankly, I doubt Bill was very worried about the support I would need after the press conference—because he had met greater needs of mine years earlier when I was giving my first foundation speeches.

One of those early speeches was especially frightening to me. Bill and I were both scheduled to make remarks at the Convention Center in Seattle. I was very uncomfortable speaking about our foundation's work in those early days, and *especially* uncomfortable speaking in front of Bill. So I told him, "Look, I really want to do this, but I'm super nervous and I don't want to give my talk in front of you, so I need you to leave after you speak."

I laugh when I think back on it, but I was not joking. I knew what I needed! So Bill gave his remarks, discreetly left the hall, got in the car, drove around for fifteen minutes, came back, picked me up, and drove us home. And he didn't make me feel even a tiny bit embarrassed that I asked him to leave. I never made that request again, but sometimes I told him, "Look, no matter how badly I'm doing, I want you to look like you're awed by every word." I was very open with him about how vulnerable I felt, and he never teased me or took advantage of my insecurities. Bill never thought my early feelings of inadequacy had anything to do with my innate ability. He could see the person I was becoming, and he almost always gave me the support I asked for.

There was one time, though, when it wasn't enough to ask for his help. I had to push.

A few years ago, Bill and I spent an afternoon with Jimmy and Rosalynn Carter at their home in Plains, Georgia. A few days afterward, Bill and I were reading books on a beach vacation, and Bill was enjoying Jimmy's *A Full Life: Reflections at Ninety*. He started chuckling, and I said, "What's so funny?" Bill said, "You want to know what caused the biggest fight in their marriage in the last twenty years?" I said, *"Yes, I do!"* I was super eager to hear it because they've been married seventy years and I wanted to know all their secrets. Bill said, "Their biggest fight came when they tried to write a book together."

I threw my head back in laughter and said, "That makes me feel so much *better*!" The first time Bill and I sat down to write our Annual Letter together, I thought we were going to kill each other. I felt, "Well, this just might end the marriage right here."

It started in the fall of 2012, when Bill was beginning work on the Annual Letter that would come out in early 2013. Bill had begun writing an annual letter about the foundation's work five years earlier. Warren had encouraged us both to do it, but I didn't feel I had the time then, with three young kids still at home. In 2007, our daughter Phoebe was just getting started in school, Rory was 8, Jenn was 11, and I was busy with other foundation work, so I didn't join Bill in writing the letter that first year or in the years that followed. He didn't suggest it. I didn't think of it. But by 2012, I had become much more active in the foundation, both behind the scenes and in public. That was the year of the London Family Planning Summit, the launch of our movement to increase access to contraceptives to 120 million more women. Naturally, as Bill began drawing up the topics he wanted to address in the letter, family planning was one of them.

I was feeling a keen sense of ownership over this issue, and Bill knew that and supported it. Although we'd agreed that we would not split our duties at the foundation and would both be engaged in all the issues, each of us would take the lead in certain areas based on our knowledge and interest. Family planning was something we agreed I would lead at the time. So if Bill was writing about that in the Annual Letter, shouldn't we be writing the letter together, or shouldn't I write that piece of it?

It's true that the Annual Letter had become Bill's project, but it was going out on foundation letterhead, through foundation channels, to foundation partners, and he was writing about a foundation project. So I could make a strong case that I should write it with him. There were arguments on his side as well, though, and I had to ask myself—"Do I want to make an issue of this?"

Eventually, I decided I had to bring it up. I didn't know what would come of it. I didn't even know what I was going to recommend, but it was bothering me enough that I knew it was wrong not to raise it. So Bill and I sat down to talk.

I told him I believed I understood things from his side. I listed all the reasons why he would feel he should write the letter on his own. But I also told him that a lot of the ideas he was going to be writing about were ideas that he and I had learned together, that had come about through the trial and error of the foundation's work and the successes of our partners in the field. Then I made a more sensitive point. I told him that there are some issues where my voice can make an impact, and in those cases, I should be speaking—separately or along with him. It strengthens my voice, it enhances our partnership, and it advances our goals.

Those were the points I made in our discussion. (I probably didn't raise them as calmly as I'm making it sound!) Bill said that the process we had for the Annual Letter had been working well for the foundation for years, and he didn't see why it should change. It got hot. We both got angry. It was a big test for us—not about how you come to agreement, but about what you do when you can't agree. And we took a long time to agree. Until then, we simmered.

In the end, Bill asked me to write a piece on contraceptives to be included in the letter. So the Annual Letter for 2013 was headlined "2013 Annual Letter from Bill Gates" and included an essay under my name covering my trip to Niger and Senegal and the London summit.

The next year's Annual Letter was headlined "2014 Gates Annual Letter" and was about "Three Myths That Block Progress for the Poor." Bill wrote about two of the myths. I wrote about one.

The next year's Annual Letter was headlined "2015 Gates Annual Letter—Our Big Bet for the Future—Bill and Melinda Gates."

That completed the evolution of the Annual Letter from his into ours.

There were so many things we did that helped us move forward, and the Annual Letter was a big one, but if I could point to one thing Bill said that captures his deep and intuitive support of an equal partnership, it came a number of years ago when a person close to us asked me if I was the "time cop" in the family. My answer was yes. I *was* the time cop. I had spent *years* making sure everything in the house got done, that the kids got dressed, did their homework, and showed up where they needed to be. But things had shifted a fair bit since the early days when that was my duty alone. The kids began to take more responsibility, and so did Bill. So I asked our friend to put that question to Bill to see what he'd say. His answer was subtler than mine, and wiser.

He said, "We try not to have anybody be the time cop for somebody else. We certainly talk about the calendar, but we never want to have something where one of us is cast in the carefree role and the other is in this bothersome role. Better to have it as a mutual challenge."

That was one of the most affirming messages I've heard from Bill about equal partnership. We try to share the roles, especially the disagreeable ones. We try to make sure we don't make one person do the dirty work. One of the defining features of hierarchy is that you take the powerful and exciting jobs for yourself and impose the crummy tasks on others. That's a *purpose* of hierarchy. So when you come together to share the unpleasant work, it's an attack on hierarchy. Because what's the point of hierarchy if it's not getting someone else to do what you don't want to do? What is hierarchy but a way to escape your share of the responsibilities?

I've been surprised when I've sometimes found friends assuming that Bill's and my marriage would have traditional gender roles because of Bill's role at Microsoft, but he and I have worked hard to shed any hierarchy except for a natural, flexible, alternating hierarchy based on talent, interest, and experience. We've agreed that our various roles in life, past or present, should have no effect on an equal partnership in our marriage, or at the foundation.

## I Take It Personally

This is the most personal chapter in the book for me, and I found it painful to write. I'm a private person, which I guess is another way of saying I'd rather keep some things to myself so I won't be judged. There were times when I decided to include something in the book and then was alarmed when I printed it out and reread it. But I've left everything in—for two reasons. First, I believe that women gain equality not couple by couple but by changing the culture, and we can change the culture by sharing our stories. That's why I'm sharing mine.

Second, I'm sharing my stories because it seems false to me to work on issues in the world while pretending I have them solved in my own life. I need to be open about my flaws or I may fall into the conceit of thinking I'm here on earth to solve other people's problems.

My friend Killian is my teacher in this. I told you about Killian earlier. Her organization, Recovery Café, serves people suffering from homelessness and mental health challenges, and everyone at Recovery Café puts mutually liberating relationships at the heart of their work. Staff, volunteers, and members all participate in small groups that practice knowing and loving each other deeply.

Killian says, "To be known without being loved is terrifying. To be loved without being known has no power to change us. But to be deeply known and deeply loved *transforms* us."

She writes about this in her book *Descent into Love*. Trying to help others while keeping them at a safe distance cannot truly help them or heal us. We have to open up to others. We have to give up the need to be separate and superior. *Then* we can help. Working on ourselves while working for others is the inner and outer work—where the effort to change the world and the effort to change ourselves come together.

Killian's insight helped me realize that a big part of the work I do to support women and girls has to be my *inner* work—facing my own fears and flaws. She helped me see that I cannot stand for gender equality in the world unless I have it in my marriage.

I've never held the view that women are better than men, or that the best way to improve the world is for women to gain more power than men. I think male dominance is harmful to society because *any* dominance is harmful: It means society is governed by a false hierarchy where power and opportunity are awarded according to gender, age, wealth, and privilege—not according to skill, effort, talent, or accomplishments. When a culture of dominance is broken, it activates power in all of us. So the goal for me is not the rise of women and the fall of man. It is the rise of both women and men from a struggle for dominance to a state of partnership.

If the goal is partnership between women and men, why do I put so much emphasis on women's empowerment and women's groups? My answer is that we draw strength from each other, and we often have to convince ourselves that we deserve an equal partnership before we get one.

The initiative cannot come only from the man's side. If it could, it would have already. A man who is dominant is probably not going to say, "Hey, let's be equal, take some of my power." But a man might respond to the changing views of other men, or to a woman who asserts her power. Change comes when men see the benefits of women's power—not just what women can do that men cannot, but a quality of relationship that comes in an equal partnership that cannot come in a hierarchical relationship: a sense of bonding, of belonging, of community, solidarity, and wholeness born of a promise that I will help you when your burdens are high, and you will help me when your burdens are low. These forces create the most rewarding feelings in life—an experience of love and union that is not possible or available to partners who struggle alone. It can turn a hierarchical relationship into an equal one, and it comes from women asserting themselves. That is why we women have to lift each other up—not to replace men at the top of the hierarchy, but to become partners with men in *ending* hierarchy.

# CHAPTER SIX

# When a Girl Has No Voice

## *Child Marriage*

On a trip I took nearly twenty years ago to see some of the harshest realities of poverty, I arrived by car at a train station in India. But I wasn't there to catch a train; I had come to meet the head of a school. It seems a strange place to meet a school head, except that's where the school was—in the train station, on the platform. The school was called a train platform school because that's where it held its classes.

Throughout India there are children who live in and around train stations. Most have run away from abusive homes, and all are very poor. They get money by collecting bottles, scavenging for coins, and picking pockets. Train platform schools are set up to offer an education to these children. The directors of this particular school also ran several shelters, trying to get the children back into their homes whenever possible, and arranging for medical help when the kids were sick. For me, meeting those kids who make their way through the day with very little money or food was a stinging rebuke to the old myth (sadly not yet dead) that the poor are not resourceful, creative, or energetic. These children and their teacher were among the most inventive people I've ever met.

The school head greeted me as I got out of the car, and I was immediately taken aback by her manner. She was very high-strung and talked in a high-pitched, fast-paced voice. She must have seen something in my response, because she said, "I'm sorry I'm so agitated. I'm not usually like this. I just got back from rescuing a girl whose family was selling her into prostitution."

That morning she'd had a call from a man who heard a girl screaming in the house next door. The child was being badly beaten—not by her father but by her husband. She was a child bride who had been given to her husband in a forced marriage. The man who heard the screams then heard the girl's husband saying that he planned to sell her. That's why the neighbor had called the school head, and she had just gone to pick up the girl and bring her in.

I asked her why the husband was beating the girl. She explained to me that the girl's family had given the dowry they had been asked to give, but the groom's family decided that the dowry wasn't enough, and they went back to ask for more. The bride's family didn't have more money, so the groom's family got angry and began beating the daughter-in-law. "It happens all the time," she said.

That was my first experience with the trauma and tragedy of child marriage.

It's hard to capture in a line or two the damage child marriage does to girls, families, and communities. But let me characterize the dangers this way. Equal partnership in marriage promotes health and prosperity and human flourishing. It invites respect. It elevates both partners. And nothing is further from equal partnership than child marriage. In all the ways that equal partnership is elevating, child marriage is degrading. It creates a power imbalance so vast that abuse is inevitable. In India, where some girls' families still pay dowries (even though dowries are illegal), the younger the girl is, and the less educated she is, the lower the dowry her family often pays to marry her off. In these cases, the market makes it clear that the more powerless the girl is, the more appealing she is to the family that receives her. They don't want a girl with a voice, skills, or ideas. They want an obedient and defenseless servant.

Girls who are forced into marriage lose their families, their friends, their schools, and any chance for advancement. Even at the age of 10 or 11, they are expected to take on the duties of housework—cooking, cleaning, farming, feeding the animals, fetching wood and water—and soon after that, they're expected to take on the duties of motherhood. The burdens of work, pregnancy, and childbirth have dire consequences for the child bride.

Many years after I first heard about child marriage, I visited a fistula hospital in Niger and met a 16-year-old girl named Fati. Fati had been married at 13 and got pregnant right away. Her labor was long and arduous—and even though she was in horrible pain and needed the care of a skilled attendant, the women in her village just told her to push harder. After three days of labor, she was taken by donkey to the nearest clinic, where her baby died and she learned she had suffered a fistula.

An obstetric fistula typically develops during a long and

obstructed labor, usually when the baby is too big or the mother too small for a smooth delivery. The baby's head puts pressure on the surrounding tissues, restricts blood supply, and creates a hole between the vagina and the bladder or the vagina and the rectum. This can lead to incontinence, including stool passing through the vagina. The husbands of girls with fistulas are frequently upset by the foul smell and the physical injury and often just kick their wives out of the family.

The best prevention for obstetric fistula is to delay the first pregnancy and have skilled attendants at the birth. Fati did neither. Instead, after being forced into child marriage and forced into pregnancy, she was forced out of her house by her husband for a condition she did nothing to cause. She lived in her father's house for two years until she was able to go to the hospital to have the fistula repaired. I had a chance to talk to her there, and I asked her what she hoped for. She said her greatest hope was to be healed so she could return home to her husband.

Meeting Fati and hearing about the abused child at the train platform school were part of my early and very incomplete education on child marriage, an education that accelerated sharply when I met Mabel van Oranje in 2012, just a few days after meeting Fati.

Mabel was one of the women who joined the dinner I mentioned earlier on the night of the London Family Planning Summit. All the women around the table talked about different issues related to women and girls, and Mabel talked about child marriage.

Mabel, I learned before the dinner, was the wife of Prince Friso, son of Queen Beatrix of the Netherlands. Her status gives a high profile to her work for human rights, but her activism began long before she married. In college, she sat in on the United Nations Security Council debates on genocide and became an intern at the UN. She started her first organization before she left university and spent the next decade advocating for peace.

As CEO of The Elders, a group founded by Nelson Mandela that brings together global leaders to push for human rights, Mabel traveled extensively. On one of her trips she met a young mother who still looked like a child. She asked the mother how old she was when she married, and the girl didn't know—between 5 and 7, she thought. Mabel was horrified, and she began using her experience, resources, and connections to learn about child marriage and launch fresh efforts to end it.

That's how she came to be at the dinner with me that night in London. I was highly impressed with her, even more so because she maintained her public work in the middle of personal tragedy. Five months before our dinner, Mabel's husband had been trapped in an avalanche while skiing and was buried under a mountain of snow. It cut off his oxygen and put him in a coma. That summer when I met Mabel, she was spending time with her husband at the hospital and helping her children through their trauma while still working as much as she could on behalf of her causes. A year later, her husband died without ever having regained consciousness.

When Mabel and I talked that night in London, she was leading an organization called Girls Not Brides, formed to end child marriage by changing the social and economic incentives that drive it. That is a huge challenge. At the time Mabel and I met, there had been more than 14 million child marriages every year for the previous ten years. One in three girls in emerging economies was getting married before her eighteenth birthday. One in nine was getting married before her *fifteenth* birthday.

Mabel was the first person who showed me the connection between family planning and child marriage. Child brides are often under intense pressure to prove their fertility, which means that their use of contraceptives is very low. In fact, the percentage of women using contraceptives is lowest where the prevalence of child marriage is highest. And low use of contraceptives by girls is deadly: For girls age 15 to 19 around the world, the leading cause of death is childbirth.

That night Mabel got my attention and became my teacher.

From the conversations at that dinner, I began to see the many ways all the gender issues were connected, and I decided I had to learn more about each area. I left the dinner with a big earful on child marriage and a keen curiosity to know more. Ordinarily, I learn about an issue by first immersing myself in it—meeting and talking to people who live with the realities that I want to understand. Then I go back and do a deeper study of the data and talk with experts and advocates. In this case, though, I did the reverse. I started with the data. And I learned that child brides have much higher rates of HIV than their unmarried counterparts. They're more likely to be raped and beaten by their partners. They have lower levels of education than unmarried girls. They are more likely to have a greater age difference with their husbands, which magnifies the power imbalance and often leads to more abuse.

I also learned that many communities that practice child marriage also practice female genital cutting. I've mentioned this practice before, but it is deeply connected to early marriage. In cultures where it's practiced, a girl's genitals are cut to make her "marriage ready." Different communities practice different types of cutting. The most severe involves not only cutting off the clitoris but sewing the vagina shut so it can be reopened when the girl gets married. Once a girl's genitals have been cut, her parents can start looking to marry her off.

Whether or not a girl is cut, a child bride's wedding night is an intense mix of pain and isolation. One Bangladeshi girl remembers that her husband's first words to her were "Stop crying."

If the girl's husband lives in a different village, then she may go with him to a community where she knows no one. Some child brides have their faces covered on the journey, so they can't find their way back home if they run away.

Child brides are targets for abuse. A study of women in several Indian states found that girls who were married before their eighteenth birthday were twice as likely to be threatened, slapped, or beaten by their husbands.

As the years pass, a child bride is likely to have more and more children—perhaps more than she can afford to feed, educate, and care for. With so many children, she has no time to earn an income, and the early pregnancies leave her body weak. This puts her at risk of being poor and sick for the rest of her life, and perpetuating that cycle of poverty for her children.

## Meeting the Married Children

These are facts I learned from the experts, but I felt I also needed to talk with some child brides and meet with people working to end this custom. So in November 2013, when I was in Ethiopia for a conference, I traveled to a remote village in the north of the country to see the work on child marriage being done by the Population Council.

When we arrived at the village, two other women and I were invited into a courtyard that was a gathering place for the village; it had a tiny health clinic, a fire pit, and a small church where we would meet. There were very few people around. We brought no staff. The men with us were asked to stay back at the car. We wanted to have the best chance to hear from the girls, so we left behind anything and anyone we thought might put them off.

We entered the church, which was very dark inside with only a few small windows letting in the light. There were about ten girls seated inside, and when my eyes adjusted to the darkness, I saw just how small they looked. They were tiny, like little fragile baby birds, still growing up, who hadn't even started to sprout their wings, and they were being married off. I wanted to put my arms around them and hug them and protect them. They were 10 or 11 years old—the age of my daughter Phoebe. But they looked even younger. Half the girls were married, I was told, and half were still in school.

I talked first to the married girls. They were so soft-spoken I could barely hear what they were saying. Even the translator had to lean in to hear. I asked them how old they were when they became brides and how they found out they were going to be married. One of the girls, Selam, told us that one day when she was 11 years old, she was helping her mother prepare for a party. She spent the whole day cooking, cleaning, and fetching water. As she told us the story, she kept pausing to take a big gulp of air, and then would continue in a whisper, as if she were telling us a secret.

As soon as the guests arrived, she said, her father took her aside and told her that she was about to be married. This was her wedding night.

That sent her into a panic. She rushed to the door and fought with the lock. She was desperate to get out of the house, to escape and run away. But her parents were ready. They pulled her back and made her stand silently next to her husband for the ceremony. When the party was over, she left her childhood home to travel to a village she had never seen, move in with her husband's family, and take on her lifelong household duties.

Each of the girls had a terribly sad story, and the saddest were ones like Selam's, in which the girls were tricked into thinking they were going to a party. Why would you trick a girl unless you knew you were breaking her heart? Several of the girls cried when they talked of their wedding day. It wasn't only that they were leaving their families and friends and moving in with strangers and cooking their meals and cleaning their homes. They had to leave school, and each of them knew what that meant. One of the brides—who looked about 8 years old—told me that school was the only path out of poverty, and when she married, the path closed. And they all told us their stories in a whisper. It's hard to capture the silence and weakness in their posture, their physical presence. Some of the girls—I remember two in particular—seemed to be just shells of themselves. They seemed so defeated. They had completely lost their voices, and I didn't see how they would ever get them back.

I tried to hide my feelings as I was listening. I didn't want to convey to the girls that I thought their lives were tragic, but that's what I was thinking, and I'm sure I showed it. I just kept getting more and more emotional. When they cried, I teared up, too—even though I tried not to.

Then I talked to the girls who hadn't been married, who were still in school, and those girls spoke a little louder. They had some confidence, and when they talked of child marriage, I could even hear a bit of defiance in their voices. It was so clear in that moment that the girls who'd been married had been robbed of something essential—as if their growth ended when their marriage began.

When we finished our visit and stepped outside, the light blinded me. I had to squint for a few moments before I could make my way across the courtyard to talk to the mentors. They were trying to help the young girls avoid marriage and help the married girls stay in school.

They were doing important work and seeing promising results. But I never do a good job absorbing the details of program work right after seeing the suffering firsthand. There's a voice in my head that says, "How can any program overcome what I just saw?" There is little useful thinking I can do on a problem right after I've seen its impact. The emotions are just too overwhelming.

On our way to the airport, we were supposed to stop for tea and debrief with the team, but I couldn't do it. I was quiet on the trip back. When we arrived at the place we were staying for the night, I took a long walk and tried to take it all in.

Earlier in the day, as I was listening to the girls, I felt nothing but heartbreak. After I got some time and distance, I started to feel angrier and angrier for the girls who were tricked into coming to their wedding. No child deserves that.

In India, as in Ethiopia, there are programs working to combat child marriage that rescue girls before they're married. The United Nations Population Fund published the story of a 13-year-old girl in the state of Bihar who overheard her parents talking about a wedding the next day. *Her* wedding.

It was a shock to her. But it was normal in her community, and in almost any other instance, the story would have unfolded like Selam's story—the girl would have resisted, but nothing would have changed. This story had a different ending. The girl in India had an app on her phone called Bandhan Tod, meaning "break your shackles." When she heard her parents talking about her wedding, she grabbed her phone, opened the app, and sent out an SOS—a child marriage distress message—that was picked up by leaders of the organizations that make up the Bandhan Tod network. A worker rushed to the girl's home and spoke to the parents. Child marriage is illegal in India, which gives the partners the leverage they need to intervene in a family event. The parents refused to back down. So the group leaders took the next step. They contacted the local police. The next day the deputy superintendent of police led a team of officers to the site where the wedding was under way. The police stopped the ceremony before it was complete, and the 13-year-old bride-to-be returned to her family home and continued in school.

It's easy for me to feel happy for the girl who escaped her wedding and returned to her family and her school. But the story itself shows how complicated the problem is, and why we need deeper solutions. Many girls being married off don't have cell phones. They don't have support networks. They don't have a local police force that will come and stop the wedding. But also, and more important, when a young girl gets out of her marriage and goes back home, she goes back to the mother and father who wanted to marry her off. How is that going to work out? She has no power in that household. She thwarted her parents, perhaps shamed them. Do her parents take out their anger on her?

It's important to be able to save girls from marriage, but it's more important to address the incentives that prompt parents to marry off their underage daughters in the first place.

When a family can receive money for marrying off a daughter, they have one fewer mouth to feed and more resources to help everyone else. When a family has to pay to marry off a daughter, the younger the girl, the less her family pays in dowry. In both cases, the incentives strongly favor early marriage. And every year a girl doesn't marry, there's a greater chance that she will be sexually assaulted—and then considered unclean and unfit for marriage. So it's also with the girl's honor and the family's honor in mind that parents often marry their girls young, so they can avoid that trauma.

Let me pause and say what a heartbreaking reality it is that girls are forced into the abusive situation of child marriage to protect them from other abusive situations. The World Health Organization says that one in three women has been beaten, coerced into sex, or abused.

Gender-based violence is one of the most common human rights abuses in the world. It's also the most obvious and aggressive way men try to control women—whether it's rape as a tool of war, or a husband beating his wife, or men in workplaces using sexual violence or bullying to belittle women who are gaining power.

I've heard nauseating stories of women who have given up their dreams because they fear for their safety, who go to worse schools that are closer to home in order to avoid sexual predators. These stories come from all over the world, including the US. Until the day we end all gender-based violence, we need stronger efforts to protect women and girls. There is no equality without safety.

In the case of early marriage, the social options of girls are so constrained by the culture that parents who marry off their girls often believe they are doing the best they can for their daughters and families. That means that fighting child marriage by itself isn't enough. We have to change the culture that makes child marriage a smart option for the poorest families.

## A Quiet Hero

Molly Melching has spent her life proving that point. Molly is another one of my teachers. I told you about her earlier. We met in the summer of 2012, and she showed me one of the best approaches I've ever seen for challenging long-standing cultural practices.

I joined Molly in a town in Senegal, and we drove out together to a rural area to see the community empowerment program she runs there. As we spent an hour or so on the drive, Molly told me about coming to Senegal as an exchange student to refine her French in the 1970s. She quickly fell in love with the Senegalese people and culture—so much so that she decided to learn the local language, Wolof, as well.

Even while she loved the country, though, she noticed how difficult it was to be a girl there. Many girls in Senegal have their genitals cut very young—usually between 3 and 5 years of age. Many are married very young and are encouraged to have children quickly and often. Outside groups had tried to change these practices, but no one succeeded, and Molly found herself in a position to see why.

She became a translator for development programs, serving as the link between villagers and outsiders who wanted to help. She quickly saw that there was more than a language barrier dividing these two groups. There was an *empathy* barrier. The outsiders showed little skill in projecting themselves into the lives of the people they wanted to help, and they had little interest in trying to understand why something was being done in a certain way. They didn't even have the patience to explain to villagers why they thought something should change.

On our drive out, Molly explained to me that the empathy barrier stymies all efforts in development. Agricultural equipment that had been donated was rusting out, health clinics were sitting empty, and customs like female genital cutting and child marriage continued unchanged. Molly told me that people often get outraged by certain practices in developing countries and want to rush in and say, "This is harmful! Stop it!'" But that's the wrong approach. Outrage can save one girl or two, she told me. Only empathy can change the system.

That insight prompted Molly to launch an organization called

Tostan and develop a new approach to social change. No one from her organization would tell a villager that something they were doing was wrong or bad. In fact, Molly told me that she never uses the term "female genital mutilation" because it's heavy with judgment, and people won't listen to you if you're judging them. She uses "female genital cutting" because it doesn't offend the people she wants to persuade.

## The Subtle Art of Change

Tostan's approach is not to judge from the outside but to discuss from the inside. Trained facilitators fluent in the local language live in the village for three years and guide a community-wide conversation. They host sessions three times a week, several hours each, and the process begins by asking people to come up with their ideal village, their so-called Island of Tomorrow. Everything Tostan does is geared toward achieving the future the villagers say they want.

To help the villagers achieve that future, facilitators teach about health and hygiene. They teach reading and math and problem solving. And they teach that every person has fundamental rights—to learn and to work, to have their health, to voice their opinions, and to be free from discrimination and violence.

These rights were far from reality even where they were being taught—particularly in communities where a woman speaking in public was considered a "good reason" for her husband to hit her. The idea that men and women were equal seemed absurd. But over time the women could see how certain changes—men doing "women's work," women earning an income—were moves toward equality, and those changes were helping. People were healthier. More of them could read. Maybe there was something to this idea.

After lessons on fundamental rights and the equality of men and women, the class started talking about women's health. It was taboo to even talk about female genital cutting—a practice they considered so old and sacred it was simply called "the tradition." Even so, the facilitator laid out its health consequences, including the risk of infection and hemorrhaging. She was met with stony silence.

At the next class, however, the village midwife raised her hand and stood up. Her heart racing, she said she'd seen firsthand how women who were cut had more difficult births. Then other women started sharing their stories, too. They recalled the pain it caused them when they were cut, the way their daughters lost so much blood, the deaths of some girls from hemorrhaging. If all girls had a right to their health, wouldn't cutting violate that right? Was it something they *had* to do? They debated intensely for months. Finally, they decided that when the time came to cut their daughters that year, they wouldn't do it.

Molly had moments like that in mind when she named the organization Tostan, a Wolof word that refers to the instant a baby chick pierces through its shell for the first time. The English translation is "breakthrough."

As Molly recalls, "We were witnessing something so significant—the act of people coming together to collectively reflect on their deepest values, to question if current attitudes and behaviors were, in fact, violating those values."

To me, that is a sacred act.

But Molly faced a challenge. She was seeing the culture of the village change, but she was worried the change wasn't going to hold. The people from this village married other people from many surrounding villages. Marrying outside their villages was a source of strength for all of them, a chance to build ties and form a larger community. But if the other villages kept the practice of female genital cutting and insisted on it for marriage, then the village Molly was working with would be isolated; its young people might find no marriage partners, and they'd probably return to the practice. Somehow, all the villages had to agree—none could change all alone.

The imam in the village and Molly discussed this worry, and he said that change needed to happen. "I will get this done," he said.

He went out for many, many days on a walking tour, visited all the villages, and spent time sitting, listening, and talking to people about girls and marriage and tradition and change. Molly didn't hear from him for a long time. Then he returned and said, "It is done." He had convinced all the villages to abandon female genital cutting—all together and all at once. In that region of Senegal, parents no longer faced a choice between cutting their daughters or forcing them to live as outcasts.

The movement quickly spread to other villages, and even other nations—led in large part by villagers whose lives the program had touched. Before long, people were questioning other harmful practices, too.

In one Senegalese village where Tostan had created a program, parents had forced their daughters to marry when they were as young as 10. People there began talking in their Tostan class about how early marriages were affecting girls. Soon after these talks began, one woman who was separated from her husband learned that he had arranged for their daughter to be married. The daughter's name was Khady, and she was 13 years old. The husband sent a representative to Khady's seventh-grade class to pull her out of school and explain that she was going to be married the next day and wouldn't be returning.

That night, her mother struck back, organizing a special meeting with the leaders of her Tostan program and the head of the elementary school. They talked long into the night. The next morning, dozens of community members and students from the school launched a march, carrying handmade signs: KEEP GIRLS IN SCHOOL and WE DON'T ACCEPT CHILD MARRIAGE.

It worked. Khady stayed in school. And the mother sent a message to Khady's father telling him that in their village, child marriage was not allowed. Khady's rescue was more powerful than the police rescue I described earlier. The police rescue was a matter of law. This rescue was a change of culture.

Today, 8,500 communities where Tostan works have promised that girls will not become child brides. According to Tostan, more than 3 million people in eight nations have said that they will no longer practice female genital cutting.

These were some of the stories Molly told me as she and I rode together to the village to talk to the people who'd brought about these changes. When we arrived, Molly and I got a raucous welcome and were invited to join a Senegalese dance. Then the imam offered a prayer, and the group held a village meeting to explain the approach of Tostan: The people in the group make all their decisions together based on their vision for the future and the rights of everyone.

After the meeting I got a chance to meet with people one-on-one. They couldn't wait to talk about how their lives had changed. The women stressed how the men had started to do chores that used to be considered women's work, like getting wood, taking care of the children, and fetching water. So I wanted to talk to the men about why they were willing to change, since the old ways seemed to serve them. "Why are you pulling water up from the well?" I asked a man after he and I had been talking for a while. He said, "It's backbreaking work. Men are stronger; men should do it. But also, I don't want my wife to be so tired. Our women were tired all the time, and when my wife isn't so tired, she's happier and our marital bed is happier."

I've told that story around the world, and it always gets a laugh.

When I talked to the women, I asked them how they got along with their husbands. One woman said, "Before, we didn't speak to our husbands, and now we are friends. Before, they beat us, and now they don't." Most of the women said that they were using contraceptives and their husbands were supportive. And the imam said, "When you have children one after the other, it's not good for your health. God would be happier if the children were healthier."

The men and women both explained how they used to marry off their daughters around age 10, but now they wouldn't do it until their daughters turned 18, even if they were offered money. I asked one of the young unmarried men if he would marry a girl under 18 from another village, and he told me he had already refused an offer to marry a girl under 18, even though he didn't know if she would still want him when she grows up.

After meeting with several larger groups, I was invited into a home with a small number of women. They talked to me about cutting; the room was dark, and the air was heavy with grief and regret. One of the women explained, "Our ancestors did it to us, so we did it to our girls. That was what we were supposed to do, and we never thought about it. We never learned about it. We thought it was an honor."

Another woman cried the entire time she described her role in the tradition. She took a piece of cloth that she was wearing on her head and used it to wipe the tears from her face, and she just kept wiping the tears away the whole time she spoke.

"I was not the cutter," she said. "I was more involved than the cutter. The cutter could not see the girl's face. I would hold the children down while they were cut. I needed to be strong to hold them down because it was horrible. The girls would scream and shout. I've held down girls even after they had run away. I've seen horrible things. Now we have stopped. I was highly criticized by my family when I stopped. But I told them it was God's will to stop because girls were dying and hemorrhaging. We will never do it again. I talk about stopping it now, and I talk to everyone."

When I returned to my hotel room that evening after hearing these stories, I couldn't stop crying.

## What Gives Me the Right?

I came away from Senegal with two questions: What makes To-stan work? And what gives me the right to get involved?

These questions—which I'll take up in a moment—relate to Hans Rosling's thought from chapter 1: *American billionaires giving away money will mess everything up!*

Hans had a point. I can see at least three ways a rich, inexperienced donor can mess things up. First, if a major funder enters an area and picks one approach over others, people working in the area might abandon their own ideas to pursue the funder's because that's where the money is. If this happens, instead of finding good ideas, the funder can inadvertently kill them off. Second, in philanthropy—in contrast to business—it can be hard to know what's working. The grantees and beneficiaries may, for many reasons, tell you things are going well when they're not. Unless you work objectively to measure results, it's easy to keep funding ideas that don't work. The third danger is that wealthy people can think that their success in one thing makes them an expert in everything. So they just act on instinct instead of talking to people who've spent their lives doing the work. If you think you're super smart and you don't listen to people, you can reach into areas outside your expertise and make bad decisions with big impact.

Those are some of the ways that Hans was right to be concerned about billionaires giving away money. I try to take these ideas into account in the way I work and in the questions I ask myself, especially this question:

What gives me the right, as an outsider, to support efforts to change the culture of communities I'm not part of?

Sure, I can say that I'm funding the work of local people and the insiders are taking the initiative. But the work of insiders can be opposed by *other* insiders, and I choose to back one group over another. How is this not the "I know best" arrogance of a wealthy, Western-educated outsider? How am I not using my power to impose my values on a community I know almost nothing about?

There's no denying that I hope to advance my beliefs. I believe that all lives have equal value. That all men and women are created equal. That everyone belongs. That everyone has rights, and everyone has the right to flourish. I believe that when people who are bound by the rules have no role in shaping the rules, moral blind spots become law, and the powerless bear the burden.

Those are my beliefs and my values. I believe they are not personal values but universal values, and I join battles for changing social norms when I can support a move away from a culture that makes one group dominant over others. I believe that entrenched social norms that shift society's benefits to the powerful and its burdens to the powerless not only hurt the people pushed out but also always hurt the whole.

So when a community denies its women the right to decide whether and when and whom to marry, but instead assigns a girl to a man as part of a financial transaction, taking from her the right to develop her talents and forcing her to spend her life as an unpaid domestic servant of others, then the universal values of human rights are not honored—and whenever there is a desire on the part of members of that community to stand up for girls who cannot speak for themselves, I believe it is a fair place to join the fight for women. That is how I explain my support for culture change in communities far from my own.

But how does Tostan's approach help me justify my involvement? Luckily—to protect others from my own blind spots and biases—the ideas I support need a lot more than my support to come into force. The process of changing from a male-dominated culture to a culture of gender equality must be supported by a majority of community members, including powerful men who come to understand that sharing power with women allows them to achieve goals they couldn't achieve if they relied on their power alone. That itself serves as the greatest safeguard against any overbearing bossiness from outsiders.

The change comes not from outside but from inside—and through the most subversive action possible: community members talking about actions that are commonly accepted, rarely discussed, and often considered taboo.

Why does it work? Conversation accelerates change when the people who are talking to each other are *getting better*—and I don't mean human beings getting better at science and technology; I mean human beings getting better at being human. The gains in rights for women, for people of color, for the LGBTQ community, and for other groups that have historically faced discrimination are signs of human progress. And the starting point for human improvement is empathy. Everything flows from that. Empathy allows for listening, and listening leads to understanding. That's how we gain a common base of knowledge. When people can't agree, it's often because there is no empathy, no sense of shared experience. If you feel what others feel, you're more likely to see what they see. Then you can understand one another. Then you can move to the honest and respectful exchange of ideas that is the mark of a successful partnership. That's the source of progress.

When people become better at seeing themselves in the lives of others, feeling others' suffering and easing their pain, then life in that community gets better. In many cases, we have more empathy for each other today than the people did who set the practices and traditions we now live with. So the purpose of conversations about accepted practices is to take out the old bias and add in empathy. Empathy is not the only force needed to ease suffering; we need science as well. But empathy helps end our bias about who deserves the benefits of science.

It's often surprisingly easy to find bias, if you look. Who was omitted or disempowered or disadvantaged when the cultural practice was formed? Who didn't have a voice? Who wasn't asked their view? Who got the least share of power and the largest share of pain? How can we fill in the blind spots and reverse the bias?

Tradition without discussion kills moral progress. If you're handed a tradition and decide not to talk about it—just do it—then you're letting people from the past tell you what to do. It kills the chance to see the blind spots in the tradition—and moral blind spots always take the form of excluding others and ignoring their pain.

Identifying and removing moral blind spots is a conversation that can be *facilitated* by outsiders, but it cannot be *manipulated* by them, because the people themselves are discussing their own practices and whether they serve their goals according to their values.

When communities challenge their own social norms in this

way, people who were forced to bear the pain of a practice that benefited others now have their needs recognized and their burdens eased. In the case of child marriage, a community-wide discussion based on empathy and guided by equality leads to a world where a woman's marriage is no longer forced, her wedding day is no longer tragic, and her schooling doesn't end when she's 10. When you examine old practices to take out bias and add in empathy, everything changes.

As Molly and I were leaving the village that day, I had one last conversation, this one with the village chief. He told me, "We used to take money for our girls—it was like buying and selling. It was the men who said that this is the way it is, but we did not understand what marriage is about. It should be where a woman is happy. If she doesn't want it, it won't be successful. There is no more forcing with us, no more child marriage. These things don't go with our true beliefs. We now have clear vision, whereas before we were nearsighted. Nearsightedness of the eyes is bad, but not nearly as bad as nearsightedness of the heart."

# CHAPTER SEVEN

# Seeing Gender Bias

## *Women in Agriculture*

On Christmas Day in Dimi village, a remote farming community in Malawi, everyone had gathered to celebrate the day except for one woman, Patricia, who was in a field a mile away, kneeling on the damp earth in her half-acre farm plot, planting groundnuts.

As the rest of her village shared food and festive conversation, Patricia worked with exacting care, making sure her seeds lined up in perfect double rows—75 centimeters between each row, 10 centimeters between each plant.

Six months later, I visited Patricia at her farm plot and told her, "I heard how you spent Christmas Day!" She laughed and said, "That's when the rains came!" She knew her crops would do better if she planted them when the ground was still damp, so that's what she did.

You'd think that someone with Patricia's dedication would be hugely successful, but for years, she had struggled. In spite of her painstaking work, even the basics had been out of reach for her and her family. She didn't have money for school fees for her kids, the kind of investment that can help break the cycle of poverty, or even money to buy a set of cooking pots, which can make life a bit easier.

Farmers need five things to succeed: good land, good seeds, farming supplies, time, and know-how. There were barriers standing between Patricia and every one of these things, simply because she was a woman.

For one, and this is common in sub-Saharan Africa, Malawian tradition in most communities dictates that women cannot inherit land. (Recently passed laws in Malawi give women equal property rights, but customs are slower to change.) So Patricia didn't own her plot. She paid to rent it. It was an expense, and it kept her from investing in the land to make it more productive.

Also, because Patricia is a woman, she didn't have a say in the family spending. For years, her husband decided what the family spent—and if that didn't include farming supplies for Patricia, there was nothing she could do about it.

Her husband also decided how Patricia spent her time. She did a funny impression of him ordering her around: "Go and do this, go and do this, go and do this, go and do this, all the time!" Patricia spent her days cutting firewood, fetching water, cooking meals, cleaning dishes, and caring for the kids. It gave her less time to spend on her crops or take her produce to market to make sure she got the best price. And if she wanted to hire help, laborers wouldn't work as hard for her as they would for a man. Men in Malawi don't like taking orders from women.

Remarkably, even the seeds Patricia was planting were affected by her gender. Development organizations have long worked with farmers to breed seeds that will grow bigger plants or attract fewer pests. For decades, though, when these groups consulted with leaders in the farming community, they would speak only with men, and men are focused on growing only the crops they can sell. Almost nobody was creating seeds for farmers like Patricia, who are focused also on feeding their families and who often grow nutritious crops like chickpeas and vegetables.

Governments and development organizations offer frequent sessions to train farmers. But women have less freedom to leave the house to attend these sessions, or even to talk with the trainers, who tend to be male. When organizations tried to use technology to spread information—sending tips via text message or over the radio—they found that men were the ones controlling that technology. If families had a cell phone, men were carrying it. When families listened to the radio, men were controlling the dial.

When you add it all up, you start to understand how a smart, hardworking farmer like Patricia was never able to get ahead. There was one barrier after another blocking her way because she was a woman.

## Understanding Patricia

By the time I met Patricia in 2015, I had come to understand the gender roles and biases that limited her success as a farmer. It had taken me a long time to figure it out—and it began when Warren Buffett gave the bulk of his fortune to our foundation.

Warren's gift opened up new frontiers for us at the foundation. We suddenly had the resources to invest in areas we knew were important, and where we saw huge promise, but hadn't yet entered in a big way. We're a learning foundation. If we see opportunity in an area that's new to us, we start by making small grants. We watch what happens; we try to figure things out. We look for points of leverage. Then we see if a larger investment makes sense. When Warren told us about his gift, we had been exploring a number of new areas but hadn't yet made the decision to scale up. His resources drove us forward and would soon lead us to gender equity as an important new focus of our giving.

Bill and I decided that we would use the new resources to move outside global health and begin making direct efforts to reduce poverty. "How do you help people in extreme poverty get more income?" That's the question we started with, and our first step was to learn more about how they live their lives, how they get their income now. It turns out that more than 70 percent of the world's poorest people get most of their income and their food by farming small plots of land. This combination presents a huge opportunity: If these smallholder farmers can make their farms more productive, they can grow more crops, harvest more food, enjoy better nutrition, and earn more income. In fact, we believed that helping the poorest farmers grow more food and get it to market could be the world's most powerful lever in reducing hunger, malnutrition, and poverty.

We decided to put our principal focus on Africa and Southeast Asia. Sub-Saharan Africa was the only region of the world where the crops grown per person had not increased in twenty-five years. If the world could help develop crops that could resist floods, drought, pests, and disease and deliver higher yields on the same land, life would improve for millions of people. So our strategy seemed clear: We would focus on the science, trying to help researchers develop new seeds and fertilizers that could help smallholder farmers grow more food.

That was the approach we set at the very beginning, in 2006, when Rajiv Shah, the head of our new agriculture program, attended a World Food Prize symposium in Iowa and gave a speech to top agriculture experts, explaining our hopes and asking for advice and ideas. The event called for Raj to speak and then hear responses from four eminent figures. Dr. Norman Borlaug was the first to respond. He had received the Nobel Peace Prize for launching the Green Revolution that created a surge of farm productivity and saved millions of people from starvation. The next speaker was Sir Gordon Conway, the chief scientific advisor at the UK's Department for International Development. Then Dr. Xiaoyang Chen spoke, who was president of South China Agricultural University.

By the time Dr. Chen finished speaking, the event had run long past its allotted time, and there was one person still to respond, a woman, Catherine Bertini, who had been executive director of the UN's World Food Programme. She sensed that the audience was tired of all the talking, so she came straight to the point.

"Dr. Shah, I would like to remind you of the quote from one of our founding mothers of the United States of America, Abigail Adams, who wrote to her husband while he was in Philadelphia working on the Declaration of Independence, and said, 'Don't forget the ladies.' If you and your colleagues at the foundation don't pay attention to the gender differences in agriculture, you will do what many others have done in the past, which is waste your money. The only difference will be you'll waste a lot more money a lot faster."

Catherine sat down, and the meeting adjourned.

A few months later, Raj hired Catherine at the Gates Foundation to teach us about the links between agriculture and gender.

## "They're Almost All Women"

When Catherine came on board, there was no talk at all of gender at the foundation. It wasn't anywhere in our strategy. I don't know what others were thinking at the time, but I'm embarrassed to say that I had not thought of gender in connection with our development work. I'm not saying that I missed the fact that women were the principal beneficiaries of many of our programs. Family planning was clearly a women's issue, as was maternal and newborn health. To reach more children with vaccinations, we had to target mothers with our message. The gender element in those issues was easy to see. But farming was different. There was no obvious gender aspect to it, at least not to me, and not at the start.

That began to change about the time Catherine joined Raj in a meeting with Bill and me to review our agricultural strategy. Raj introduced Catherine and said, "She's here working on gender." That word seemed to provoke Bill, and he started talking about being effective, getting results, and staying focused on that. Bill supported women's empowerment and gender equity but thought they would distract us from the goal of growing more food and feeding more people—and he thought anything that would blur our focus would hurt our effectiveness.

Bill can be intimidating, but Catherine was eager to have that conversation. "This is completely about effectiveness," she said. "We want to make smallholder farmers as effective as they can be, and we want to give them all the tools—the seeds, fertilizer, loans, labor—they need to achieve it, so it's very important for us to know who the farmers are and what they want. Next time you're in Africa driving in a rural area, look out the window and see who's working in the fields. They're almost all women. If you listen only to the men, because they're the ones with the time and social permission to go to the meetings, then you're not going to know what the women really need, and they're the ones who are doing most of the work."

Catherine left the meeting and said to Raj, "Why am I here? If he doesn't buy it, it's never going to work." Raj just said, "He heard you. Trust me."

A few months later, Catherine was driving down the road listening on her car radio to an interview Bill was doing on NPR about economic development, and Bill said, "The majority of poor people in the world are farmers. Most people don't know that the women are doing most of that work, and so we're giving them new seeds, new techniques. And when you give women those tools, they use them very effectively."

Catherine almost drove off the road.

What Catherine experienced there, which Raj predicted, is that Bill learns. He loves to learn. Yes, he challenges people very hard, sometimes too hard, but he listens and learns, and when he learns, he is willing to shift. This passion for learning is not just Bill's approach; it's mine as well. It's the central pillar of the culture we've tried to create at the foundation, and it explains how we all—some faster than others—came to agree that gender equity should drive the work we're all trying to do.

The fact that most of the farmers in Malawi are women wouldn't matter if gender differences and inequalities didn't exist. But as Patricia's life shows, gender differences and inequalities *do* matter—in ways that make it much harder for women to grow the crops they need.

Hans Rosling once told me a story that helps make the point. He was working with several women in a village in the Congo to test the nutritional value of cassava roots. They were harvesting the roots, marking them with a number, and putting them into baskets to take them down to the pond to soak. They filled three baskets. One woman carried off the first basket, another woman carried the second basket, and Hans carried the third. They walked single file down the path, and a minute later, as they all put down their baskets, one of the women turned around, saw Hans's basket, and shrieked as if she'd seen a ghost. "How did this get here?!"

"I carried it," Hans said.

"You *can't* carry it!" she shouted. "You're a man!"

Congolese men don't carry baskets.

Strict gender rules extend to other areas as well: who clears the land, who plants the seeds, who weeds the field, who does the transplanting, who runs the house, cares for the children, and cooks the meals. When you look at a farmer, you're looking at a mother. Household labor not only takes time away from farming but keeps the woman from attending meetings where she could get tips from other farmers and learn about improved seeds, best practices, and new markets. As soon as you see that most farmers are women, and that women are beneath men, everything shifts.

A landmark 2011 study from the UN's Food and Agriculture Organization showed that women farmers in developing countries achieve 20–30 percent lower yields than men even though they are just as good at farming. The women underproduce because they do not have the access to the resources and information that men do. If they had the same resources, they would have the same yields.

The report said that if we could recognize poor women farmers as clients with distinctive needs and develop technology, training, and services designed specifically for them, then women's crop yields would be the same as men's. That would put more income in the hands of women, give them a stronger voice in the household, lead to better nutrition for the children, add income for school fees, and—because of the rise in food production—reduce the number of undernourished people in the world by 100 to 150 million.

The rewards are immense, but so are the challenges. Patricia is not just one woman; she is millions of women. And those millions of women have smaller plots of land than men. They have less access to extension services, to the market, and to credit. They lack seeds and fertilizer and training. Women in some areas are not allowed to hold bank accounts or enter into contracts without the endorsement of a male family member.

If you're working to help women change their lives and you hit these gender barriers, it could make you step back and say, "Culture change is not our role." But when you learn that women are more than half of all farmers and can't get what they need to make their plots productive, and as a result their children go hungry and their families stay in poverty, it forces you to choose. You can keep doing the same thing and reinforce the biases that keep people poor. Or you can help women get the power they need to feed their children and reach their potential. It's a clear choice—challenge the biases or perpetuate them. Politically, it's a tricky question. Morally, it's easy: Do you submit to the old culture that keeps women down, or do you help create a new culture that lifts women up?

Fighting for gender equity in agriculture was never our plan. We had to spend some time trying to take it all in. That is one of the great challenges for anyone who wants to help change the world: How do you follow your plan and yet keep listening for new ideas? How can you hold your strategy lightly, so you'll be able to hear the new idea that blows it up?

We started out thinking that poor farmers just needed better technology, such as new seeds that would allow them to grow more crops on the same land in harsher weather. But the potential for a farming revolution was not only in the seeds; it was in the power of the women who plant them. This was the huge missed idea. This was the new plan. If we want to help farmers, we have to empower women. Now, how do we get everyone on the team to see it that way?

## Whispering About "Women's Empowerment"

As I saw it at the start, the goal of empowering women was not in addition to, but on behalf of, more food, better nutrition, and higher income for the poorest people in the world.

Gender equity is a worthy goal for its own sake. But that was not how it was going to be sold in our foundation. Not back then. This was a new idea, and there were skeptics. One highly placed person shut down a conversation by saying, "We don't do 'gender.'" Another person pushed back, "We are *not* becoming a social justice organization!"

When we started, we were mindful of the resistance. Even the most passionate advocates wouldn't talk about empowerment. That term put people off and obscured the core message, which is "you have to know what the farmer needs." We simply had to remind people working on agriculture that the farmers were often women. That meant that the researchers had to start gathering information from women, not just men. It meant that the scientists working on new seeds needed to talk to women.

Here's an example. When agricultural researchers want to improve a new rice seed, they often leave their labs and go talk to the farmers about the traits they want to see in an improved seed.

This is a great idea. But many of the researchers are men, and they often talk only to male farmers. The woman farmer very often isn't part of the conversation because she is too busy on other tasks in the household, or because it's culturally inappropriate for a male professional to speak with a woman, or because the researcher doesn't realize how critical her input is.

Often, then, what happens is that the researchers tell the men about the traits of an improved seed, and the men like what they hear. So the researchers go back to the lab and finish the seed and help get it to market. The men buy it, and the women plant it, and then the women (who do most of the harvesting) see that the rice stalk grows too short, and they have to stoop over to harvest it.

After a while, the women tell their husbands they want a taller plant that doesn't break their backs during harvest. So the farmers don't buy the seeds anymore, and a whole lot of time and money and research has been wasted that could have been saved if only someone had talked to the women.

The good news is that the International Rice Research Institute (IRRI) has learned that women and men farmers have some differences in what they're looking for in a good rice variety. Both men and women prefer traits like high yield; obviously, they want to produce more crops if they can. But because women's jobs on the farm include harvesting and cooking, they also prefer rice varieties that grow to the right height and don't take as long to cook. So the IRRI researchers make a point of talking to men *and* women when they consult with farmers on the traits they want in the improved seeds. They know that if input from both men and women is included in seed development, farmers are more likely to adopt that seed in the long run.

Once we were armed with these lessons, we began to make grants that could break down the barriers women farmers faced in getting the improved seeds, fertilizer, and technology—and the loans—they needed to be productive on the farm.

One of the early grants we made was beautifully simple: We wanted to get technical assistance to farmers in rural Ghana, so our partner decided to air a radio show telling women farmers how to grow tomatoes, and they did a lot of research to make sure the show would have the greatest possible reach. They'd decided on radio as the best medium because many people couldn't read and most people had no TV. Once a week was the right pacing, since it lined up with the pace of new tasks for the growers. Tomatoes were the best crop because they were relatively easy to grow, and they were a cash crop that would also improve nutrition for the family. The last thing they had to figure out was what time women listened to the radio—because if they put the program on when the man controlled the radio, the woman wasn't going to learn a thing about growing tomatoes.

That's the kind of thinking that began to take hold in the foundation; people became very tuned in to gender differences and social norms in programs where they mattered. We began the shift in a low-key way, with just a few gender experts at the foundation talking to people who wanted to hear how a gender focus could help them achieve their goals. And they spoke softly. One of the early leaders, Haven Ley, who now is my top policy advisor, jokes that she "worked in the basement for three years." She scarcely ever said the words "gender equity" or "women's empowerment." Instead, she explained to people how paying attention to gender differences would make an impact. "You can't just come in there and talk about your concerns," Haven says. "No one cares. You have to figure out what success looks like to people, what they're scared about failing at, and then you can help them get what they want."

Progress was steady, but it was too slow for me. People were still speaking softly about gender at the foundation, sometimes in whispers, not quite wanting to come forward. I could see how even some of the strongest advocates were tiptoeing around it, how in meetings they'd raise it but not push it—careful not to say too loudly what they knew to be true.

For an agonizingly long time, I couldn't give them the lift I wanted to give them. I was watching, but I was not ready. It wasn't the right time. The foundation wasn't quite ripe; my command of the data wasn't good enough. I didn't have the time to take on a huge new project—I was working hard on family planning. I had three kids at home. I was figuring out equality in my own marriage. There were so many things in the way. But then the moment came and the timing was right. I was ready. I had the conviction, the experience, and the data at hand. The foundation had the staff. So I decided to write an article for the September 2014 issue of *Science* in which I would set out our foundation's commitment to gender equity.

In the article, I acknowledged that we at the foundation were latecomers in using gender equity as a strategy. "As a result, we have lost opportunities to maximize our impact," I wrote. But our foundation would now "put women and girls at the center of global development," because "we cannot achieve our goals unless we systematically address gender inequalities and meet the specific needs of women and girls in the countries where we work."

I wrote the article for our partners and for funders and others involved in the work. But principally, I wrote it as a message to everyone who works at the Bill & Melinda Gates Foundation. I felt the need to state loudly and publicly our strategy and priorities on gender equity. It was the strongest lever I ever pulled to direct the focus and emphasis of our foundation. It was time to move out of the basement.

## Lifting Each Other Up

Six months after the *Science* article ran, I took a trip to Jharkhand, a state in eastern India, to visit a grantee of ours called PRADAN.

PRADAN was one of the first organizations we invested in after we saw the central role of women farmers.

When PRADAN began its work in the 1980s, its leaders didn't start with a focus on empowering women; they figured it out as they went along. In the spirit of *pradan*—"giving back to society"—the group began placing committed young professionals in poor villages to see if they could help out. When the new recruits arrived in the villages, they were shocked to see how the men treated the women. Husbands would beat their wives if they left home without permission, and everyone—even the women—thought that was acceptable. Naturally, these women had no standing in the community: no resources, no bank accounts, no way to save, and no access to loans.

So leaders at PRADAN began talking to the husbands, getting permission for their wives to meet in groups of ten or fifteen to talk about farming. The deal with the husbands was "if you let your wife attend these groups, she'll increase your family's income." So the women began to meet regularly and save their money together, and then, when one of them needed to make an investment, she could take out a loan from the group. When the group got enough money, it would connect with a commercial bank. This helped a great deal with the financial aspects of farming. But the women soon also demanded the same agricultural training the men got. They learned how to identify the seeds and grow the crops that would allow them to feed their families, sell the surplus, and make it through the hunger season.

That was the background of the group, so when I attended a meeting, I was prepared to be impressed, but even I was surprised when the group leader said, "Raise your hand if—before you joined the self-help group—you could grow enough food to last your family the full year."

Not a single hand went up.

Then she said: "Raise your hand if you had a surplus to sell last year."

Almost every hand went up.

Empowerment never confines itself to categories. When farming advice and financial support began to make a difference for the women, they started looking for new battles to fight. When I visited, they were lobbying to get better roads and clean drinking water. They'd recently put in an application with the local government for the village's first toilets. They'd started a campaign against their village's alcohol abuse problem—calling on the men to stop drinking, pressuring government officials to enforce the laws, and even working with the local women who sell alcohol to help them find new ways to make a living.

And there was another sign of empowerment—the way the women carried themselves. When I meet women who've faced heavy gender bias, I often see it in the way they look at me. Or don't look at me. It's not easy to unlearn a lifetime of being meek. The posture of these women was different. They stood tall. They spoke up. They weren't afraid to ask questions, to tell me what they knew, what they thought, what they wanted. They were activists. They had that look. They had been lifted up.

The empowerment approach taken by PRADAN is central to our foundation's strategy. We help connect women to people who can advise them on farming and connect them to markets. We also help women access financial services so they can save money and get loans. When women get the money for their work deposited into their own bank accounts, they earn more and save more. They also are more respected by their husbands, and that begins to shift the power in the household.

This is the kind of work we've been accelerating since I wrote that article in *Science,* and we've changed the foundation so we can pursue it. We've hired more gender experts. We're getting data on the lives of women and girls so the things that matter get measured. And we're supporting more organizations like PRADAN that take an overt and intentional approach to empowering women. Increasingly, we are seeing the results that come from putting women and girls at the center of our strategy.

## Patricia's Breakthrough

Patricia, the farmer who was planting her seeds on Christmas Day, saw her life changed by the empowerment that came through membership in a group. Let me tell you the rest of her story.

Patricia joined a program called CARE Pathways, an organization that teaches conventional farming tips but also teaches farmers about equality. The group asked Patricia to get her husband to join the sessions, and she was a bit surprised and gratified when he agreed. In one session, Patricia and her husband were told to role-play their life together at home but to switch places—the wife would play the role of the husband, and the husband would play the role of the wife, just like the exercises I described in the chapter on unpaid work. Patricia got to order her husband around, just as he'd been doing to her: "Go and do this, go and do this, go and do this!" And her husband had to do what she said without complaint.

The exercise opened his eyes. Afterward, he told her he realized that he hadn't been treating her as a partner. In another exercise, they drew the family budget like a tree, with roots representing their sources of income and branches representing expenditures. They discussed together which roots could get stronger and which branches could get pruned. As they discussed Patricia's farm income, they talked about her farming supplies, and whether maybe they should be a higher priority.

Patricia told me these exercises changed her marriage. Her husband began listening to her ideas and working with her to help make her farm plot more productive. Soon after the sessions, an opportunity came that made all their decisions pay off.

CARE Pathways, concerned that there weren't very many quality seeds for the kinds of crops women tend to grow, began working with a local research station to design a groundnut seed that produces more nuts and does a better job resisting pests and disease. They developed a good seed, but they didn't have nearly enough seeds to supply them to all the women farmers in the area. They first needed to find farmers to grow these seeds into plants that produce more of these perfected seeds. Only after the seeds had multiplied enough could they be sold to other farmers.

This process is called "seed multiplication," and it requires even more care and attention than typical farming. Only the best farmers are selected to be seed multipliers—and Patricia became one of them. When I asked her how she could produce at the high level needed to be a seed multiplier, she said, "I have a supportive husband now."

That supportive husband agreed that he and Patricia should take out a loan to buy the improved seeds. That's what Patricia was planting on Christmas. By the time I met her, she'd had her first harvest. The half-acre plot produced so much that she could supply seeds to other farmers and still plant two full acres of her own the following season, four times what she'd planted the year before. And from that harvest came not only plenty of food for her family but enough income to cover her children's school fees and also pay for those cooking pots!

## Women Are Inferior; It Says So Right Here

Farming is not the only area of the economy that is stunted by gender bias. Recent reports from the World Bank show that gender discrimination is encoded in law nearly everywhere in the world.

In Russia, there are 456 jobs women cannot perform because they're deemed too strenuous or dangerous. Women there can't become carpenters, professional divers, or ship captains, to name just a few positions. One hundred and four countries have laws that put certain jobs off-limits for women.

In Yemen, a woman can't leave the house without her husband's permission. Seventeen countries have laws that limit when and how women can travel outside the home.

In Sri Lanka, if a woman is working in a shop, she must stop by 10:00 P.M. Twenty-nine countries restrict the hours women can work.

In Equatorial Guinea, a woman needs her husband's permission to sign a contract. In Chad, Niger, and Guinea-Bissau, a woman needs her husband's permission to open a bank account.

In Liberia, if a woman's husband dies, she has no right to her family's assets. She herself is considered part of his property—and, as people in some rural communities will explain, "property cannot own property." Thirty-six countries have rules limiting what wives can inherit from their husbands.

In Tunisia, if a family has a daughter and a son, the son will inherit twice as much as the daughter. Thirty-nine countries have laws that keep daughters from inheriting the same proportion of assets as sons.

In Hungary, men on average are paid a third more than women in managerial positions—and this does not violate the law. In 113 countries, there are no laws that ensure equal pay for equal work by men and women.

In Cameroon, if a wife wants to earn additional income, she has to ask her husband's permission. If he refuses, she has no legal right to work outside the home. In eighteen countries, men can legally prohibit their wives from working.

Finally, discrimination against women is perpetuated not only in laws that exclude women but also in the absence of laws that support women. In the United States, there is no law ensuring paid maternity leave for new mothers. Worldwide, there are seven countries where women are not guaranteed paid maternity leave. The ideal, of course, would be paid leave for any major family health situation, including parental leave for new dads. But the lack of paid maternity leave—and paid parental leave—is an embarrassing sign of a society that does not value families and does not listen to women.

Gender bias does worldwide damage. It's a cause of low productivity on farms. It's a source of poverty and disease. It's at the core of social customs that keep women down. We know the harm it causes and the good that comes from defeating it—so how should we fight it?

Should we fight it law by law, sector by sector, or person by person? I would say "all of the above." Also, instead of just working to undo the disrespect, we should find the *source* of the disrespect and try to stop it there.

## Discrimination Against
## Women—Seeking the Source

An infant boy at his mother's breast does not disrespect women. How does that feeling get hold of him?

Disrespect for women grows when religions are dominated by men.

In fact, some of the laws I mentioned above are based directly on scripture, which is why it is so difficult to undo them. It's not a standard political debate when an argument for equality is called blasphemy.

Yet one of the strongest statements I've seen on the danger of male-dominated religion comes from a man steeped in religion. In Jimmy Carter's book *A Call to Action: Women, Religion, Violence, and Power*, he calls the deprivation and abuse of women and girls "the most serious and unaddressed worldwide challenge," and he lays the principal blame on men's false interpretation of scripture.

It's important to remember when taking in Carter's message that he is a passionate and dedicated lifelong Baptist who has been teaching Sunday School at his Maranatha Baptist Church in Plains, Georgia, since 1981. His life-saving, ground-breaking work over four decades at the Carter Center is a testament to the power of his faith to inspire acts of love. It's especially notable, then, that Carter would write the following:

"This system [of discrimination] is based on the presumption that men and boys are superior to women and girls, and it is supported by some male religious leaders who distort the Holy Bible, the Koran, and other sacred texts to perpetuate their claim that females are, in some basic ways, inferior to them, unqualified to serve God on equal terms. Many men disagree but remain quiet in order to enjoy the benefits of their dominant status. This false premise provides a justification for sexual discrimination in almost every realm of secular and religious life."

It would be impossible to quantify the damage that has been done to the image of women in the minds of the faithful as they've attended religious services over the centuries and been taught that women are "unqualified to serve God on equal terms."

I believe without question that the disrespect for women embodied in male-dominant religion is a factor in laws and customs that keep women down. This should not be surprising, because bias against women is perhaps humanity's oldest prejudice, and not only are religions our oldest institutions, but they change more slowly and grudgingly than all the others—which means they hold on to their biases and blind spots longer.

My own church's ban on modern contraceptives is just a small effect of a larger issue: its ban on women priests. There is no chance that a church that included women priests—and bishops and cardinals and popes—would ever issue the current rule banning contraceptives. Empathy would forbid it.

An all-male, unmarried clergy cannot be expected to have the empathy for women and families that they would have if they were married, or if they were women, or if they were raising children. The result is that men make rules that hurt women. It is always a temptation when you're making rules to put the burden on "the other," which is why a society is more likely to support equality when "the other" is not just sitting next to you at the table as you write the rules, but actually writing them *with* you.

The Catholic Church tries to shut down the discussion of women priests by saying that Jesus chose men as his apostles at the Last Supper, and therefore only men are allowed to be priests. But we could as easily say that the Risen Christ appeared first to a woman and told her to go tell the men, and therefore only women are allowed to bring the Good News to the men.

There are many possible interpretations, but the Church has said that the ban on women priests has been "set forth infallibly." Putting aside the irony of leaving women out of the leadership of an organization whose supreme mission is love, it's demoralizing that men who make rules that keep men in power would be so unsuspicious of their own motives.

Their claims might have been more convincing in past centuries, but male dominance has lost its disguises. We see what's happening. Some parts of the Church come from God, and some parts come from man—and the part of the Church that excludes women comes from man.

One of the weightiest moral questions facing male-dominated religions today is how long they will keep clinging to male dominance and claiming it's the will of God.

Encouraging the voices of women of faith is not an explicit part of my philanthropic work. But the voice of male-dominant religion is such a cause of harm—and the voice of progressive religious leaders is such a force for good—that I have to honor the women who are challenging the male monopoly and are amplifying female voices to help shape the faith.

But women can't do it alone. Every successful effort to bring in outsiders has always had help from insider activists who do the work of reform from within. Women need male allies. They know this, and so in every religion where men have unequal influence, women are raising questions that make men uneasy. Who are the men who will stand with the women? And who are the men who will keep quiet out of obedience to rules they know are wrong?

The number of Catholic priests I've talked to who support ordaining women, combined with the institutional Church's absolute opposition to women priests, convinces me that morally, in some cases, institutions are less than the sum of their parts.

It may strike you as a little odd that a chapter that opens with gender in farming would close with a discussion of religion, but we have a duty to trace women's disempowerment up the stream to its source. Women around the world who are trying to reshape their faith, who are wresting the interpretation of scripture from the grip of a male monopoly, are doing some of the most heroic work for social justice and economic opportunity in the world today. They're on the edge of a new frontier. These women and their male allies, especially the men working for reform inside ancient institutions, deserve our gratitude and our respect.

# CHAPTER EIGHT

# Creating a New Culture

*Women in the Workplace*

Much of my work is focused on helping women and families get out of poverty because that's where I feel I can make the biggest impact. I also want all women to be able to develop our talents, contribute our gifts, and flourish. Gender equality benefits all women, no matter our level of education, privilege, or accomplishment, in the home or the workplace.

Women in the workplace is a vast topic. So much has been said and written on it that it's impossible to know it all, and yet most of us know the issues personally because we've lived them. I'm sharing here my experiences in a workplace and industry that I know well, drawing some lessons that apply broadly, hoping to sketch the outlines of the workplace of the future where women will be able to flourish *as ourselves* without sacrificing our personalities or personal goals. I'm giving special emphasis to my time at Microsoft because the stories I will tell you from those days formed many of my views on the workplace—and also because the tech industry has disproportionate power to shape the future.

One of the most influential figures in my professional life was a woman I met only once. During spring break of my last year at Duke, I flew home to Dallas to pay a visit to IBM, where I had worked several summers during college and grad school. I had an appointment with the woman I'd be working for if I took IBM's offer of a full-time job, which I expected to do.

The woman greeted me warmly, offered me a seat in her office, and, after a few minutes of courteous conversation, asked me if I was ready to accept her offer. I was a bit more nervous than I expected when I said, "Actually, I have one more place I plan to interview with, this small software company in Seattle." She asked if I would mind telling her which one, and I said, "Microsoft." I began to tell her that I still expected to take IBM's offer, but she cut me off and said, "If you get a job offer from Microsoft, you *have* to take it."

I was stunned. This woman had spent her career at IBM, so I had to ask, "What makes you say that?" She said, "The chance for advancement will be incredible there. IBM's a great company, but Microsoft's going to grow like mad. If you have the talent I think you have, the chance you will have there to advance as a woman will be meteoric. If I were you and they made me an offer, I would take it."

This was a pivotal moment for me, and it's one of the reasons

I'm a passionate advocate for women in tech—I want to pay forward the generosity of my mentors and role models.

When I flew into Seattle for my interviews, I was still pretty sure I would go back and work at IBM. Then I met some of the people at Microsoft. One of the more memorable guys greeted me with drumsticks in his hands and drummed his way through our whole interview—on his desk, on the walls, all over his office. It wasn't something he did with just women; it was something he just did. I had to raise my voice to be heard, but he was listening. I thought it was kind of funny, actually, and eccentric. You can get away with eccentric if you're great at what you do, and it seemed everyone I met was great.

I loved the pulse, the electricity, of the place. Everyone was so passionate about what they were doing, and when they talked about their projects, I had a feeling I was seeing the future. I had written a lot of code in college, and I loved it, but this was a much higher plane for me. I was like a girl playing youth soccer meeting the US Women's World Cup Team. I loved hearing them talk about how people were using their products, what they hoped to do next, how they were changing the world.

At the end of the day, I called my parents and said, "My gosh, if this company offers me a job, I will have to take it. There's just no way I can't take it."

Then I went off to spring break with friends in California, and my parents went off to the library to look up this Microsoft company. My mom and dad were excited about the idea that I might come back home to Dallas and work, but they always said they wanted me to go where adventure and opportunity led me. That's the path they took. I want to take a moment here to tell you about them, how they met, and how I learned from them to follow my dreams.

My parents both grew up in New Orleans. My dad's father owned a machine shop, which in the 1940s was focused on making machine parts for the war effort. The shop's profits were the sole income for the family, and my grandparents didn't have a dime to send my dad to college. Luckily, though, my dad attended a Catholic school run by the Christian Brothers, and a Brother there became his mentor and kept telling him, "You have to go to college." The word of a Brother carried weight in my dad's house. So the fall after my dad graduated from high school, his parents put him on a train to Georgia Tech in Atlanta with his newspaper route earnings and a jar of peanut butter.

Once in college, my dad split his time between studying in Atlanta and working in Dallas, where he got a job with an aerospace company. That's how he earned the money to put himself through college, and that's how he eventually ended up working at LTV Aerospace on the Apollo program.

When my dad came home to New Orleans for Christmas after his first quarter at Georgia Tech, two Dominican nuns decided he needed a date during the holidays—Sister Mary Magdalen Lopinto, who was a mentor of my dad's and had given him jobs during high school, and Sister Mary Anne McSweeney, who was my mom's aunt. (She was very significant in my life. I called her Auntie growing up. She taught me how to read, and I remember trying on her habit once when I was little!) The sisters were best friends, and they were amused that my father had recently had two girlfriends who *both* left him for the convent. My great-aunt, Sister Mary Anne, told her friend about my mom, who for a while had attended a juniorate high school as a candidate for the sisterhood. They decided she was the one for my dad.

Sister Mary Magdalen called my dad and said, "You don't have any girlfriends anymore. You sent them both off to the convent. So we're going to send you to this house on South Genois Street, and you will meet a girl, Elaine, who's already been to the nunnery and come out, so you won't lose her the way you lost the others."

So my dad went to South Genois Street and met my mom.

She said, "They called me and asked me if I would be willing to go out with this guy whom I'd never met, and I thought, *Well, he can't be too bad if nuns are suggesting that I date him.*"

A few days later they went out for a date on *The President*, a big multi-deck boat with a stern paddlewheel that cruised up and down the Mississippi River. It must have gone well. They dated for five years while my dad was in college. Then my dad got a scholarship to do graduate work in mechanical engineering at Stanford, so they got married and drove out to California, where my mom, who never went to college, supported them both with her income as an administrator for a company in Menlo Park. When they moved back to Dallas, my mom was pregnant with my sister, Susan, their first child, and right away my dad was working on the Apollo program and NASA was racing to land a man on the moon. My mom said that she remembers him working almost twenty-four hours a day, seven days a week. Some days he would go to work and come home three days later, getting brief naps on his office couch.

That left absolutely everything to my mom. She ran the house.

She raised four kids. And when my parents started a residential real estate investment business so they could afford to pay for us kids to go to any college we could get into, my mom ran the business during the day. My dad contributed hugely in the evenings and on weekends, no question, but my mom's to-do list every single day when she was working on the business was just unreal. How she juggled it all, I have no idea. (But I've noticed now, looking back, that for all my mom did to raise four kids and run the house, it's when my parents ran their real estate business together that they gained more equality in their marriage.)

My mom and dad knew from their own lives the pull of opportunity, and they had done their research at the library and were ready to support my move to Seattle when the Microsoft recruiter called my home and reached my mom. Mom, who is all of about five feet, with her sweet southern accent, said, inappropriately, "Oh, please can't you tell me if you're going to give Melinda a job offer?" And the recruiter said, "Well, I'm really not supposed to do that." So she put the charm on and asked him again, and he caved and said, "Well, in fact, we are going to make her an offer." So Mom jotted down the details on a small notepad (which she saved and I still have), then started calling me in California. As soon as she reached me with the message, I called Microsoft and accepted.

I was *thrilled*!

A few months later, I flew to Seattle for an orientation with my new employer. I was in Microsoft's first class of MBAs, and the company decided to have the ten of us come out for a visit and figure out which group we should join at the start. Our first session was in the boardroom—the biggest conference room they had; that's how small the company was back then, about 1 percent of the size it is today. As I looked around the table, I saw only men. That didn't seem weird; majoring in computer science in college got me used to being in rooms full of men. But then the vice president of applications marketing came in to talk, and as he was presenting, the guy sitting next to me, the same young age I was and fresh out of Stanford Business School, got in an all-out debate with this VP. This wasn't just a spirited exchange; it was a brash, escalating face-off, almost a brawl, and I was thinking, *Wow, is this how you have to be to do well here?!*

It took me a few years to get my answer.

When I started work, I realized instantly that my mentor at IBM had it right. I got opportunities at Microsoft there was no possible way I would have gotten anywhere else. Three weeks into my start, I'm 22 years old flying to New York for a meeting and I'm running the meeting. I'd never *been* to New York. I'd never even hailed a cab!

It was the same for all of us at Microsoft. We laughed about it later, but it was scary. One friend told me his manager came in and said, "I want you to figure out higher ed," and he said, "What do you mean, figure out higher ed?" and the manager said, "What do you mean, what do I mean?" It was not a place for people who needed a lot of guidance. We were climbing the mountain without a map, and we were building the mountain without instructions. And we were all madly excited about what we could help people do with software.

Our customers were just as excited as we were, so the opportunities kept coming. I started out as product manager for Microsoft Word, then became group product manager for a series of products. Then marketing manager for a larger set of products. ("Products," by the way, was the in-house term for software programs.) Then group marketing manager. Then I wanted to focus on the product, not just the marketing, so I became product unit manager for Microsoft Publisher. That involved managing teams doing the testing, development, and all the things that go into creating a product. And guess what—when you're that young and get that much opportunity, you get the opportunity to make mistakes, too, and I took full advantage of that! I was the group product unit manager for Microsoft Bob. (You don't remember Microsoft Bob?!) We hoped it would make Windows more user-friendly. It was a flop. The tech critics killed it. We'd already announced the product and knew we faced some headwinds before our first public demo. So I went onstage for that event wearing a T-shirt that said MICROSOFT BOB on the front and had a bright red bull's-eye on the back. They hit the target. I got pounded. But you just can't put a value on what you learn when you stand up as the face of a project that failed. (There was a joke in the company that you didn't get promoted until you had your first big failure. Not entirely true, but useful solace in difficult times.)

Mercifully, most of my other failures weren't as public as this one, or as painful. But all those failures were useful. In one sequence of missteps, I made the mistake of expensing something I wasn't allowed to expense. *Yikes! Not* something that a good Catholic girl who sits in the front row and gets good grades ever wants to do—especially when she's the new girl in a male-dominated company.

Not just my manager but my manager's manager came down on me. I tried to explain that I had asked an admin about the procedure. No one cared. No time for that.

Soon afterward, I was in a meeting with the same manager, and he was throwing me questions about how we should price our new product, and I didn't know a particular number—our cost of goods sold, which is a key number that a product manager should know to the penny. It's not just that I didn't know that number. That wasn't the big issue. The big issue was that I didn't understand my customers well enough to know what they would be willing to pay. I learned that, from that point on, I needed to know the key numbers—and I'd darned well better know where they came from and why they're important.

After that meeting, I thought, *Wow, I may not survive. This is the top manager in my area. I'm one of the few women, I messed up on my expense report, and I misstepped on this.* I remember asking a few people, "Can I ever regain this guy's trust?" It took me a while, but I rebuilt my relationship with him, and I ended up better off than if I had expensed things properly and knew the number he'd asked for. Nothing sharpens my focus like a mistake.

All these experiences and opportunities made me see why the IBM manager urged me to take the job. It was exhilarating and challenging, and I was learning a ton, but something about it wasn't right for me. A year and a half into the job, I started thinking about quitting.

It wasn't the work or the opportunities; they were awesome. It was the culture. It was just so brash, so argumentative and competitive, with people fighting to the end on every point they were making and every piece of data they were debating. It was as if every meeting, no matter how casual, was a dress rehearsal for the strategy review with Bill. If you didn't argue strenuously, then either you didn't know your numbers or you weren't smart or you weren't passionate. You had to prove you were strong, and this is how you did it. We didn't thank each other. We didn't compliment each other. As soon as something was done, we took little time to celebrate. Even when one of the best managers left the company, he just sent out an email saying he was leaving. There was no party, no group good-bye. It was weird. Just a speed bump as we raced through our day. That was the standard of how you had to be to succeed there—and it felt pervasive in the company. I could do it. I did do it. But it was draining, and I was getting tired of the rough-and-tumble. *Maybe I should go work for McKinsey,* I thought. McKinsey is a top management consulting firm known for driving its people hard—but not compared to what I was living at the time. I had interviewed with them before accepting the job at Microsoft, and they had called me a few times to check in on me and ask me if I liked where I was. So I nursed that escape fantasy for months, but I couldn't make myself do it because I really loved what I was doing at Microsoft. I loved building products, I loved staying ahead of the curve, I loved knowing what users needed even before they did— because we saw where tech was going and we were taking it there.

The truth was that I loved the mission and vision of Microsoft, so I said to myself, "Maybe, before I leave this amazing place, I should see if I can find a way to do all the things that are part of the culture—stand up for myself, know the facts, have a spirited debate—but do it in my own style." From the beginning, instead of being myself, I had been acting in the style of men I perceived were doing well in the company. So the question came to me like an epiphany: Could I stay at the company and be myself? Still be tough and strong, but also say what I think and be open about who I am—admitting my mistakes and weaknesses instead of pretending to be fearless and flawless, and above all finding others who wanted to work the way I did? I told myself, "You're not the only woman in this company, and you can't be the only person trying on a false personality to fit in." So I looked for women and men who were having the same trouble with the culture that I was.

What I realized much later, paradoxically, is that by trying to fit in, I was strengthening the culture that made me feel like I *didn't* fit in.

## Creating Our Own Culture

I started by reaching out more intentionally to other women in the company, seeking support for the way I wanted to be at the firm. The friend I leaned on most was Charlotte Guyman. Charlotte and I met about eight weeks into my time at Microsoft. I remember the day vividly because the day I met Charlotte was also the day that I met my future father-in-law. We were all at the American Bar Association Conference in San Francisco, where Microsoft had a trade booth, and Charlotte and I were both scheduled to be working there, demonstrating Microsoft Word.

She and I were in different work groups, but we were both told to figure out how Microsoft Word could break into the legal market, where our competition, Word Perfect, had a 95 percent market share. Charlotte was in a new group called channel marketing, and she was trying to market all our products to a given customer set, in this case the legal community. I, on the other hand, was the Word product manager trying to market Microsoft Word to any market. So Charlotte and I were coming at the same goal from two different directions. With some people, that could have turned competitive, but with Charlotte, it wasn't that way at all. As soon as we realized we had this shared assignment, we opened up to each other: I'll do this, you do that, and we'll both do this third thing together. It worked perfectly because we both wanted the same result and we didn't care about who got credit—we just wanted Microsoft to win.

I arrived at our trade booth first, all abuzz because I loved doing the demo for Word. Then Charlotte showed up, and we were all energy and excitement. I've heard that you never actually meet a great friend; you *recognize* her. That's how it was with Charlotte. We were instant friends. We had a blast doing the demos, watching each other's style, learning a ton. Later in the day we spotted Bill's dad in the hall. He wasn't hard to pick out; he's six foot seven. He walked right up to me and I did the product demo for him. I was amazed at how lighthearted he was and how easy he was to talk to, how he made everyone around him comfortable. (Bill and I weren't dating yet, so I didn't know the significance of our meeting!)

Overall, I had a fantastic day. It always was that way with Charlotte. In retrospect, I realized that the core of my new effort to become comfortable at the firm was to try to work with everyone in the same way I worked with Charlotte. Arms and heart wide open.

(Charlotte not only wanted to work the same way I did; she had a striking way of critiquing the culture. She once said, "It's not okay for women to cry at work, but it's okay for men to *YELL* at work. Which is the more mature emotional response?")

As I began to see how I might be myself in the Microsoft culture, I found a group of women who wanted to work the same way I did, and also some like-minded men. By far the most important guy friend of mine was John Neilson. I mentioned John earlier. He was one of my best friends in life, who would die before he turned 40. He and Emmy came with Bill and me on that first trip to Africa in 1993, and John and I responded to that trip in the same way, as we did to so many things. We were both very social people, we'd probably both be called "sensitive" by our colleagues, and we bonded through our efforts to be a part of the culture at Microsoft and also bring some empathy to the work. John was a vital support for me, and I hope I was the same to him. Years later, when I first heard the term "male ally" as a phrase for men who were passionate advocates for women, I thought, *That was John.*

Connecting with other women and creating our own culture had payoffs beyond anything I'd dreamed of. Charlotte has remained one of the closest friends of a lifetime. John and Emmy Neilson were best friends with Bill and me. Then Charlotte introduced me to Killian, who had just moved to Seattle from Washington, DC, and would found Recovery Café in 2003. Killian is deeply passionate about community and the spiritual life. Her faith tells her to include the excluded, and she brings that faith to life more than anyone else I've ever met. When she arrived, she encouraged the conversation the four of us were eager to have. "Okay, when you have more than you need at a material level, what's next? Where do we go from here? Where do our gifts connect with a need in the world? How do we use our lives to build up our larger human family?"

Charlotte, Emmy, Killian, and I started jogging together every Monday morning as soon as we got our kids to school. Then we decided to add some friends, all women, and form a slightly larger group with a spiritual focus. There are nine of us, and we've been meeting on the second Wednesday of the month for almost twenty years now, reading books, taking trips, going on retreats, exploring ways of putting our faith into action. Our Monday jogging foursome is still intact, too, though we do more walking than jogging these days, and try not to dwell on what that might mean!

Every friend I made helped change the culture of the workplace for me, but if I had a breakthrough moment in becoming myself at Microsoft, it was when Patty Stonesifer became my boss and mentor and role model. (As I mentioned earlier, Patty was so trusted and respected by Bill and me that we asked her, as she was leaving Microsoft, if she would become the first CEO of our foundation, which she was for ten spectacular years.) Patty was seen as a star early on at Microsoft. She had her own style, and people flocked to work for her. Her group was a place where people came and wanted to stay because they felt very supported. We could be honest about what our strengths and weaknesses were, about the challenges of growing some new and difficult categories of business. Nobody knew the answers, and if we pretended we knew, we weren't going to make any progress. We had to be willing to try stuff, kill things that didn't work, and try something new. And we began to grow a strain of the Microsoft culture that was always there, but we gave it emphasis, and that was the ability to say "I was wrong." It was amazing to be able to admit weaknesses and mistakes without worrying that they would be used against us.

Working for Patty, I began to develop a style that was really my own, and I stopped suppressing myself to fit in. That's when I fully realized that I could be myself and be effective. The more I tried it, the more it worked. And it shocked me. As I moved up, and eventually was managing 1,700 people (the whole company was 1,400 people when I started and about 20,000 when I left in 1996), I was getting software developers from all over the company who'd been there for years, and people would say, "How did you get those stars to come work for you?" I got them because they wanted to work in the same way I did.

I found the guts to try it out because I saw it work for Patty, and that's the power of a role model. She encouraged me to be true to my own style, even if she didn't know she was having this effect on me. Without Patty, I never would have been able to accomplish the goals I set for myself—not then and not since.

In the midst of my reinvention, probably because life has a sense of humor, I became friends with the Stanford recruit who started the brash exchange with the VP during our orientation visit. One night when we were with a group of friends for dinner, I asked him, "Do you remember that time in the MBA orientation, where you had this all-out brawl with the VP? I couldn't believe you did that. I know you now, and it just doesn't seem like you."

He turned completely red—embarrassed as he could be—and said, "I can't believe you remember that. The truth is, I had an organizational behavior professor in business school who had just told me the week before that I wasn't assertive enough and I should try to be bolder. So I was trying it out."

That was a lesson for me. Men also face cultural obstacles in the workforce that keep them from being who they are. So anytime women can be ourselves at work, we're improving the culture for both men and women.

That's how I turned things around for myself at Microsoft— being myself and finding my voice with the help of peers, mentors, and role models. Being yourself sounds like a saccharine prescription for how to make it in an aggressive culture. But it's not as sweet as it sounds. It means not acting in a way that's false just to fit in. It's expressing your talents, values, and opinions in your style, defending your rights, and never sacrificing your self-respect. That is power.

## Careful, She's Tougher Than You Think

If I had to summarize the lessons I learned at Microsoft, where I started work more than thirty years ago, it's that I reported to a woman who supported my efforts to work in my own style in a culture that rewarded results, which is why I was able to get promoted and do well. If I had tried to do it on my own without colleagues who encouraged me and a boss who supported me, I would have failed. The backing I got at Microsoft a generation ago was something all women should have today. But even now, some women get the opposite. I want to tell you the story of one.

Before I do, I want to be open about something that concerns me. One of the challenges of writing my stories *and* telling other people's stories is the risk that I might be seen to be suggesting some equivalence between my stories and theirs. I think the best way to manage that risk is to state flat out that the challenges of the people I highlight in this book far outstrip mine. That's why they're in the book. They're heroes of mine. I'm certainly not equating my efforts to prosper in the Microsoft culture with the efforts of other women to survive and withstand the trials of their workplaces. For so many women in the workplace, "being yourself" is a much tougher challenge than what I faced at Microsoft.

Here's a story from the world of technology that is far different from mine.

When Susan Fowler started her new job at Uber in 2016, her manager sent her a series of messages trying to talk her into having sex with him. As soon as she saw the messages, she thought that this guy had just gotten himself in trouble. She took screenshots of the conversation, reported him to HR—and learned that *she* was the one in trouble. HR and upper management told her that this guy "was a high performer," it was his first offense (a lie), and Susan had a choice: She could switch to a new team or stay and expect a poor performance review from the guy she'd reported.

Susan had grown up in a rural community in Arizona, one of seven children of a stay-at-home mom and a preacher who sold payphones on weekdays. She was homeschooled, so at 16 she started cold-calling colleges and asking what she needed to do to get in. While working as a nanny and a stablehand, she found out how to take the ACT and SAT and submitted a list of books she'd read to Arizona State. They gave her a full scholarship.

Susan eventually transferred to the University of Pennsylvania to study philosophy and to take more science classes—but administrators tried to keep her from taking physics because she'd had only sixth-grade-level math. She wrote a letter to the university president asking, "Didn't you give a speech saying Penn is here to help us fulfill our dreams?" Susan won the support of the president and began teaching herself all the math she'd missed out on and then took graduate-level physics courses.

That's the woman Uber hired. And some of her bosses expected to be able to abuse her and lie to her and suppress her efforts to speak up for herself, but it didn't work out that way. Susan's attitude, as she later told *The New York Times'* Maureen Dowd, was "No. You don't get to do that."

Susan transferred to another department, found a new role at Uber she loved, and started receiving perfect performance reviews. But then, because her new manager needed to keep some token women on his team, he began adding hidden negative performance reviews so Susan couldn't get promoted out of his group. She asked about the negative reviews, and no one would explain them. The reviews not only kept her from pursuing the work she wanted, but they affected her bonus and take-home pay, and made her ineligible for Uber's sponsorship in a Stanford graduate program she loved.

Susan began filing a report with HR every time she experienced something sexist. Eventually, her manager threatened to fire her for reporting incidents to HR. And Susan and other women endured gratuitous slights, like the company ordering leather jackets for all the male employees but not ordering them for the female employees because, they said, there were so few women at Uber that the company couldn't get a volume discount.

Meanwhile, women were transferring out, and the percentage of women in Susan's organization dropped from 25 percent to 6 percent. When she asked what was being done about the plunging number of women, she was told that the women of Uber needed "to step up and be better engineers."

In one of her last meetings with HR, the rep asked Susan if she ever considered that maybe *she* was the problem.

When Susan decided to leave Uber, she had a job offer in a week. But after she left, she still faced a decision. Should she forget it or should she speak out? She knew that going public with sexual harassment charges could define people for the rest of their lives, and she worried about that. But she also knew many women at Uber who'd had similar experiences, and if she spoke out, she'd be speaking for them too.

Susan came down on the side of "No. You don't get to do that." She wrote a 3,000-word blog post on her year of being abused. The day she posted, it went viral. The next day, Uber hired former attorney general Eric Holder to investigate. After Holder submitted his report, Uber's CEO was forced to resign, and twenty other people were fired. Soon other women in the tech sector began speaking out, and there were more firings and new policies. One headline said, SUSAN FOWLER'S UBER POST WAS THE FIRST SHOT IN A NEW WAR AGAINST SILICON VALLEY SEXISM.

A few months later, the war spread beyond tech and a few other industries when the Harvey Weinstein scandal broke. Women from around the country shared stories of sexual harassment and abuse with the hashtag #MeToo. We adopted activist Tarana Burke's phrase "Me Too"—which Tarana used in 2006 to build a community of sexual assault survivors—and took it viral. In just twenty-four hours, there were 12 million posts on Facebook alone.

At the end of 2017, Susan was on the cover of *Time*'s Person of the Year issue along with other prominent women of the #MeToo movement. The magazine called them the "Silence Breakers."

The women who came forward and spoke up should be celebrated and their numbers expanded. But we also need to support women who are in blue-collar jobs and service-sector jobs, women who don't have access to social media, whose abusers are not famous, whose stories aren't interesting to reporters, and who live from paycheck to paycheck. What are their options for fighting back? How can we help them? Every woman who speaks up is a victory—but we need to find a way to make each victory matter to the women who still have no voice.

### What Happened?

The #MeToo movement, and every woman and organization that contributes to it and emerges from it, is winning important victories for women *and* men. But it's just a start. If we want to broaden and sustain these advances, we have to understand how they happened.

*What happened?* Why did change take so long, and why then did it come so suddenly? When women hear our own voices in another woman's story, our courage grows, and one voice can become a chorus. When it's "he said/she said," the woman can't win. But when it's "he said/she said/she said/she said/she said/she said," transparency has a chance, and light can flood the places where abusive behavior thrives.

In 2017, the offenders kept lying, but their defenders gave up. They couldn't hold back the truth, and the dam broke. When women saw that more people were taking the side of the accusers over the abusers, the many stories that had been held inside came pouring out, and the abusers had to go.

When overdue change finally comes, it comes fast. But why did the abusers dominate for so long? Part of the answer is that when women are trying to decide whether we should stand up, we don't know if others will stand with us. It often takes many women, arms linked, to inspire other women to speak.

Before I met Bill, I was in an unhealthy relationship. The guy encouraged me in some ways but held me back on purpose in others. He never wanted me to eclipse him. He didn't see me as a woman with my own dreams, hopes, and gifts. He saw me as someone who could play a useful role in his life, so there were certain ways he wanted me to be, and when I wasn't that way he could be extraordinarily abusive. I'm sure that's one of the reasons I get so angry today when I see women being put down or kept in certain roles. I see myself in them.

When I started my relationship with him, I was young. There was no chance of my being myself or finding my voice at that point in my life. I was confused. I felt awful, but I didn't understand why. There were enough moments of support to make me want to overlook the abuse and dismiss the feeling that I had to get out. When I look back, it's clear to me that I had lost a lot of my voice and confidence, and it took me years to see what I had lost and get it back.

Even after it was over, I still didn't really understand what had been happening until I came to have some healthy relationships. But I never fully grasped the sick power of that abusive relationship until years after it had ended, when I went to a YWCA fundraiser for a women's and family shelter. A woman in a smart blue business suit stood at the podium and told her story, and that's the first time I ever said to myself with full understanding, "Oh my gosh. That's what was happening to me."

I believe that women who've been abused may be quiet for a time, but we never stop looking for a moment when our words will make an impact. In 2017, we found our moment. But we need to do more than identify the abusers; we have to heal the unhealthy culture that supports them.

An abusive culture, to me, is any culture that needs to single out and exclude a group. It's always a less productive culture because the organization's energy is diverted from lifting people up to keeping people down. It's like an autoimmune disease, where the body sees its own organs as threats and begins attacking them. One of the most common signs of an abusive culture is the false hierarchy that puts women below men. Actually, sometimes it's worse than that—when women are not only below men in the hierarchy but are treated as objects.

In workplaces around the world, women are made to feel that we aren't good enough or smart enough. Women get paid less than men do. Women of color get paid even less. We get raises and promotions more slowly than men do. We don't get trained and mentored and sponsored for jobs as much as men do. And we get isolated from one another more than men do—so it can take women a long time to realize that the bad fit we're feeling is not our fault but a fact of the culture.

One sign of an abusive culture is the view that members of the excluded group "don't have what it takes." In other words, "If we don't have many women engineers here, it's because women are not good engineers." It is unimaginable to me both how flawed the logic is and how widely it's believed. Opportunities *have* to be equal before you can know if abilities are equal. And opportunities for women have never been equal.

When people see the effects of poor nurture and call it nature, they discourage the training of women for key positions, and that strengthens the view that the disparity is due to biology. What makes the biology assertion so insidious is that it sabotages the development of women, and it relieves men of any responsibility for examining their motives and practices. That's how gender bias "plants the evidence" that leads some people to see the effects of their own bias and call it biology. And that perpetuates a culture that women don't want to join.

## When Men Write the Rules

It's frustrating to me that women are still facing hostile cultures in many fields today, and I'm especially upset that these issues are keeping women out of the tech industry. These are such exciting jobs. They're fun. They're innovative. They pay well. They have a growing impact on our future, and there are more of them every year. But it's more than that. Tech is the most powerful industry in the world. It's creating the ways we will live our lives. If women are not in tech, women will not have power.

The percentage of computing graduates who are women has plunged since I was in college. When I graduated from Duke in 1987, 35 percent of computing graduates in the United States were women. Today, it's 19 percent. There are likely a lot of reasons for the drop. One is that when personal computers made their way into American households, they were often marketed as gaming devices for boys, so boys spent more time on them and it gave boys exposure to computers that girls didn't get. When the computer gaming industry emerged, many developers started creating violent war games featuring automatic weapons and explosives that many women didn't want to play, creating a closed cycle of men creating games for men.

Another likely cause is the early view of the ideal computer coder as someone with no social skills or outside interests. This view was so prevalent that some employers used the hiring process to identify candidates who showed a "disinterest in people" and disliked "activities involving close personal interaction." That screened out many women.

Finally—and this shows the gender bias in our culture when it comes to who's considered fit for a task—when software engineering was seen as more clerical in nature and much easier than the hardware side, managers hired and trained women to do the work. But when software programming came to be understood as less clerical and more complex, managers began to seek out men to train as computer programmers—instead of continuing to hire and train women.

As the number of men in the sector grew, fewer women went into tech. Which made it even harder to be a woman in tech. So *even fewer* women went into tech, and men began to dominate the field.

Fortunately, there have been some encouraging shifts. The forces that made computer science into a boys' club are softening, and people in the industry are doing more to counter the gender bias. These changes may have begun moving the trend in the right direction.

Another challenge is the low percentage of women in venture capital, which is even lower than the percentage of women in the computer industry. Venture capital is a crucial source of funding for entrepreneurs who are just starting a business and can't afford a bank loan. Investors give them the capital they need to grow in exchange for a stake in the business. It can make the difference between failure and huge success.

Only 2 percent of venture capital partners are women, and only 2 percent of venture capital money is going to women-founded ventures. (The amount of venture capital that goes to firms founded by African American women is 0.2 percent.) Nobody can think this makes economic sense. Women are going to have a ton of great business ideas that men are never going to think of. Unfortunately, "Who will have the most exciting business ideas?" is not the question driving the decisions.

When you're funding start-ups, there is so little data on what works in early-stage investing that the funders give money to the people they know—guys who went to the same schools and go to the same conferences. It's an old-boys' club with younger boys. In 2018, Richard Kerby, an African American venture investor, polled 1,500 venture capitalists and found that 40 percent had attended Stanford or Harvard. When there is such a concentration of people from one group, one sector, one set of schools, the impulse to fund people from your own peer networks drives you toward a homogeneous set of firms. When you try to fund outside that network, the firm and the funder might both feel it's just not a good "fit."

That's why I'm investing now in venture capital funds, including Aspect Ventures, that invest in women-led companies and companies formed by people of color. This isn't charity on my part. I expect a good return, and I'm confident I'll get one because women are going to see markets that men won't see, and black and Latina and Asian women will see markets that white entrepreneurs won't see. I think we'll look back in ten years and see it was crazy that more money wasn't flowing toward markets understood by women and people of color.

Gender and racial diversity is essential for a healthy society. When one group marginalizes others and decides on its own what will be pursued and prioritized, its decisions will reflect its values, its mindsets, and its blind spots.

This is an ancient problem. A few years ago I read *Sapiens*, by Yuval Noah Harari. The book covers the history of human beings, including the cognitive, agricultural, and scientific revolutions. One of the things that stayed with me was Harari's description of the Code of Hammurabi, a set of laws that was carved into clay tablets around 1776 BC and influenced legal thinking for centuries, if not millennia.

"According to the code," writes Harari, "people are divided into two genders and three classes: superior people, commoners and slaves. Members of each gender and class have different values. The life of a female commoner is worth thirty silver shekels and that of a slave-woman twenty silver shekels, whereas the eye of a male commoner is worth sixty silver shekels."

One eye of a male commoner was worth twice the *life* of a female commoner. The code prescribed light penalties for a superior person who committed a crime against a slave, and harsh penalties for a slave who committed a crime against a superior person. A married man could have sex outside marriage, but a married woman could not.

Is there any doubt who wrote the code? It was the "superior" men. The code advanced their views and reflected their interests and sacrificed the welfare of the people they saw as beneath them. If societies are going to elevate women to equality with men—and declare that people of any race or religion have the same rights as anyone else—then we have to have men and women and every racial and religious group together writing the code.

This for me is the defining argument for diversity: Diversity is the best way to defend equality. If people from diverse groups are not making the decisions, the burdens and benefits of society will be divided unequally and unfairly—with the people writing the rules ensuring themselves a greater share of the benefits and a lesser share of the burdens of any society. If you're not brought in, you get sold out. Your life will be worth twenty shekels. No group should have to trust another to protect their interests; all should be able to speak for themselves.

That's why we have to include everyone in the decisions that shape our cultures, because even the best of us are blinded by our own interests. If you care about equality, you have to embrace diversity—especially now, as people in tech are programming our computers and designing artificial intelligence. We're at an infant stage of AI. We don't know all the uses that will be made of it—health uses, battlefield uses, law enforcement uses, corporate uses—but the impact will be profound, and we need to make sure it's fair. If we want a society that reflects the values of empathy, unity, and diversity, *it matters who writes the code*.

Joy Buolamwini is an African American computer scientist who calls herself "a poet of code." I learned about Joy when her research exposing racial and gender bias in tech began to get coverage in the media. She was working with a social robot some years ago as an undergraduate at Georgia Tech when—in the course of playing a game of peek-a-boo—she noticed that the robot couldn't recognize her face in certain lighting. She used her roommate's face to complete the project and didn't think about it again till she went to Hong Kong and visited a start-up that worked with social robots. The robot there recognized everyone's face but hers, and hers was the only face that was black. Then she figured out that the robot was using the same facial recognition software her robot at Georgia Tech used.

"Algorithmic bias," Joy said, "can spread bias on a massive scale."

When Joy became a researcher at the MIT Media Lab, she tested facial recognition software from IBM, Microsoft, and the Chinese company Megvii and found that the error rate for recognizing light-skinned males was below 1 percent, while the error rate for recognizing darker-skinned females was as high as 35 percent. Joy shared her results with the companies. Microsoft and IBM said that they were already working to improve their facial analysis software. Megvii didn't respond.

All you have to do is pause and reflect on the various meanings of the word "recognize" to shudder at the idea that the software is slow to recognize people who don't look like the programmers. Will the software one day tell an agent, "We don't 'recognize' this person; she can't board the plane, pay with a credit card, withdraw her money, or enter the country"? Will other programs, replicating the biases of the programmers, deny people a chance to get a loan or buy a house? Will software programmed by white people disproportionately tell police to arrest black people? The prospect of this bias is horrifying, but this is just the bias we can predict. What about the program bias that we can't predict?

"You can't have ethical AI that's not inclusive," Joy said.

African American women are only 3 percent of the entire tech workforce; Hispanic women, 1 percent. Women comprise about a quarter of the tech workforce and hold just 15 percent of the technical jobs. These numbers are dangerously, shamefully low. That's why I am so passionate about women in tech and women of color in tech. It's not just that it's the world's largest industry. Or that the economy is going to add half a million computing jobs in the next decade. Or that diverse teams in tech lead to more creativity and productivity. It's that the people in these jobs will shape the way we live, and we all need to decide that together.

I am *not* saying that women should be given positions in tech that they haven't earned. I'm saying women *have* earned them and should be hired for them.

Just about everything I needed to know about the value of women in tech I learned from a man in tech: my dad. My dad was a strong advocate of women in math and science—not just personally for his daughters but also professionally in his career. I told you about the excitement of watching the space launches with him and my family, but just as memorable for me as a kid was meeting some of the women on my dad's teams. After working on the Apollo space program, he worked on Skylab, Apollo-Soyuz, the Space Shuttle, and the International Space Station, and he recruited women very intentionally for each one of these programs. Whenever he was able to hire a woman mathematician or engineer, he shared his excitement at home with us. There weren't very many women available, he told us, and his group always did better when he could get a woman on the team.

My dad began to see the extra value of women in the 1960s and '70s. There wasn't much data to support him on this back then, but there is now—a ton of it, and it's impressive. Here's an example: A 2010 academic study on group intelligence found that the collective intelligence of a workgroup is correlated to three factors: the average social sensitivity of the group members, the group's ability to take turns contributing, and the proportion of females in the group. Groups that included at least one woman outperformed all-male groups in collective intelligence tests, and group intelligence was more strongly correlated to gender diversity than to the IQs of the individual team members.

Gender diversity is not just good for women; it's good for anyone who wants results.

### Ask for What You Need

So how do we create a workplace culture that expands opportunities for women, promotes diversity, and doesn't tolerate sexual harassment? There is no single answer, but I do believe it's crucial to gather friends and colleagues and create a community with a new culture—one that respects the larger goals of the existing culture but honors different ways of getting there.

Unfortunately, the effort to create a culture that advances the interests of women faces a challenging barrier: Research suggests that women may have more self-doubt than men, that women often underestimate their abilities while many men overestimate theirs.

Journalists Katty Kay and Claire Shipman wrote a book about this called *The Confidence Code*. Kay explained in an interview, "Women often find action harder than men because we are more risk-averse, because the fear of failure is enormous for us. It seems to be bigger than it is for men." In one example, they point to a review of personnel records at Hewlett Packard, which showed that women were applying for promotions only when they thought they met 100 percent of the job requirements, while men were applying when they thought they met 60 percent of them.

The tendency to underestimate our abilities, for those of us who may have it, plays a role in keeping us back, and it's hard not to imagine that it's a result of a male-dominated culture that seeks to marginalize women. These efforts are often indirect; they can be subtle and insidious—not attacking women directly but attacking the qualities and characteristics of women who are most likely to challenge men.

This angle seems to be supported by another line of research, one suggesting that women's reticence comes not from a lack of confidence but from a calculation. A 2018 *Atlantic* article cites a study that says women with self-confidence gained influence "only when they also displayed . . . the motivation to benefit others." If women showed confidence without empathy or altruism, they faced a "'backlash effect'—social and professional sanctions for failing to conform to gender norms." It's fear of this backlash, according to another study, that keeps women from asserting themselves.

Women may be less assertive from a lack of confidence or out of calculation, but male-dominated cultures remain a key underlying cause for both. There is social approval for women who don't ask for much, who show self-doubt, who don't seek power, who won't speak out, who aim to please.

These gender expectations have been significant for me and for many women I know because they foster qualities that lead to perfectionism—the effort to compensate for feelings of inferiority by being flawless. I should know; perfectionism has always been a weakness of mine. Brené Brown, who is a genius in stating big truths with few words, captures the motive and mindset of the perfectionist in her book *Daring Greatly*: "If I look perfect and do everything perfectly, I can avoid or minimize the painful feelings of shame, judgment, and blame."

That is the game, and I am a player.

Perfectionism for me comes from the feeling that I don't know enough. I'm not smart enough. I'm not hardworking enough. Perfectionism spikes for me if I'm going into a meeting with people who disagree with me, or if I'm giving a talk to experts who know more about the topic than I do—something that happens often for me these days. When I start to feel inadequate and my perfectionism hits, one of the things I do is start gathering facts. I'm not talking about basic prep; I'm talking about obsessive fact gathering driven by the vision that there shouldn't be anything I don't know. And if I tell myself I shouldn't overprepare, then another voice tells me I'm being lazy. Boom.

Ultimately, for me perfectionism means hiding who I am. It's dressing myself up so the people I want to impress don't come away thinking I'm not as smart or interesting as they thought. It comes from a desperate need to not disappoint others. So I overprepare. And one of the curious things I've discovered is that when I'm overprepared I don't listen as well; I go ahead and say whatever I've prepared, whether it responds to the moment or not. I miss the opportunity to improvise or respond well to a surprise. I'm not really there. I'm not my authentic self.

I remember an event at the foundation a few years ago where I got called out on my perfectionism.

Sue Desmond-Hellmann—our super-inventive foundation CEO who's a scientist, a medical doctor, and a creative leader who loves to push Bill and me (and herself)—put us on the spot by arranging an uncomfortable exercise for foundation leaders that would strengthen the bond between leadership and staff. I agreed to go first.

I sat down in a chair in front of a video camera (placed there so everyone in the foundation could later watch!) and was given a stack of cards facedown, which I was to turn over one by one. Each card had something that a foundation employee had said about me but didn't want to tell me in person. My job was to read the card and respond, on camera, so everyone could see me react. The statements were bold, especially the last one. I turned over the card and it said, "You're like Mary *F@$*ing* Poppins—practically perfect in every way!"

As my kids said to me that night at the dinner table, *"Ouch!"*

In the moment, conscious of being on camera, I burst out laughing—probably partly from nervousness, partly because it was so bold, and partly because I was delighted that someone thought I had it together. I said, through my laughter, "If you knew how much I am not perfect. I am so messy and sloppy in so many places in my life. But I try to clean myself up and bring my best self to work so I can help others bring *their* best selves to work. I guess what I need to role-model a little more is the ability to be open about the mess. Maybe I should just show that to people."

That's what I said in the moment. When I reflected later, I realized that maybe my best self is not my polished self. Maybe my best self is when I'm open enough to say more about my doubts or anxieties, admit my mistakes, confess when I'm feeling down. Then people can feel more comfortable with their own mess, and that's an easier culture to live in. That was certainly the employee's point. I need to keep working with Sue and others to create a culture at the foundation where we can be ourselves and find our voices. And when I say "we," I'm not being rhetorical. I'm including myself. If I haven't helped to create a culture in my own organization where all women and men can find their voice, then I haven't yet found *my* voice. I need to do more to become a role model for others in the way Patty was a role model for me, and Sue is today. I want to create a workplace where everyone can bring their most human, most authentic selves—where we all expect and respect each other's quirks and flaws, and all the energy wasted in the pursuit of "perfection" is saved and channeled into the creativity we need for the work. That is a culture where we release impossible burdens and lift everyone up.

## A Workplace Compatible with Family Life

A workplace that is hospitable to women will not only forgive our imperfections but accommodate our needs—especially the most profound human need, which is our need to take care of one another.

We have to create a workplace that is compatible with family life. This requires support from the top, perhaps with a push from below. The rules that shape the lives of employees in the workplace today often don't honor the lives of employees *outside* the workplace. That can make the workplace a hostile place—because it pits your work against your family in a contest one side has to lose.

Today in the US, we're sending our daughters into a workplace that was designed for our dads—set up on the assumption that employees had partners who would stay home to do the unpaid work of caring for family and tending to the house. Even back then it wasn't true for everyone. Today it is true for almost no one—except for one significant group. The most powerful positions in society are often occupied by men who *do* have wives who do not work outside the home. And those men may not fully understand the lives of the people who work for them.

As of 2017, almost half of employees in the US workforce were women, and seven of ten American women with children under 18 were in the labor force. About a third of these women with kids at home were single moms.

The old-fashioned assumption that there is a housewife at home to handle things is especially harsh for single parents. This is not just a personal problem, but a national and global problem; populations are aging—in the US and all over the world—and the task of caring for aging parents is falling disproportionately to women, which aggravates the gender imbalance in unpaid work that is already there.

When people are torn between the demands of work and home, it can steal the joy from family life. We need our employers to understand our duties to family, and we want compassion at work when a crisis hits home.

When I reflect on my time as a manager at Microsoft, I can think of so many moments when I could have done more to make the culture kinder to families. My leadership on this issue wasn't great, so I hope you'll forgive me for telling you a story of a time I got it right.

One day nearly thirty years ago, a very gifted man who had been working in my group for a year or two leaned his head into my office and said, "Do you have a minute?"

"Sure," I said. "What's up?"

"I wanted you to know that my brother is very ill."

"I'm so sorry. Can I ask with what?"

"He's got AIDS."

It took guts for him to tell me that. This was in the early '90s when there was a lot more ignorance and stigma around AIDS. I offered as much sympathy as I could, and I felt uncomfortable that I couldn't do more. He told me a bit about his brother, and when he was done saying what he had come to say, he stood up, said, "Thank you for letting me tell you," and left my office.

I pondered our conversation for a few days, and it became clear why he wanted to tell me. As I've said, Microsoft was an especially hard-charging culture at the time. It was intense and competitive. Many people didn't take vacation, most of us were unmarried, and almost none of us had kids. We were in that short period of early adulthood when almost nobody needed us, so nothing got in the way of work. And this young man was an especially high performer. So I think he was worried. He was caught between his family and his job, and he loved both. I think he was hoping that if he told me what was going on, I wouldn't hold it against him when the crisis hit and his performance dropped because he was loyal to his brother and wanted to spend time with him.

A week or so later, I saw him in the hallway and motioned him into my office. He said, "What? Did I do something?" I said, "I've been thinking—it's going to be really important for you to focus on our top ten resellers this year." This was back when software was sold through retail stores. He said, "Oh, absolutely, I'm doing that. I'll show you my list." He showed me the list; he had the re-sellers all ranked. And I said, "In particular, I think you should focus on Fry's Electronics." He said, "Oh, yeah, they're in the top ten. I'm already doing that."

He wasn't getting my point, so I said, "No, I think that Fry's is really important. It's a relationship we need to foster. Anytime you need to be down there, go ahead. I don't need to know about it. Just go."

Fry's might have been in the middle of his list. They weren't rising up or falling down, so I think he was confused by my emphasis. Then it hit him and his eyes welled up with tears. He nodded and said, "I'll do that. Thank you," and left my office.

We never spoke of it again. We didn't have to. We both knew what was happening. We were creating our own little culture. Fry's Electronics was in the Bay Area, where his brother lived. I wanted him to know he could go there anytime with the company's blessing. Long before we had a name for it, he and I were improvising paid family and medical leave.

Paid family and medical leave allows people to care for their families and themselves in times of need. We were improvising because the company didn't have a policy on paid family and medical leave, and neither did the country. Now the company does, but the country still doesn't. Let me repeat a point I made in chapter 7, and I hope others repeat it, too. The United States is one of only seven countries in the world that do not provide paid maternity leave—joining the company of Papua New Guinea, Suriname, and a handful of other island nations. This is startling evidence that the United States is far behind the rest of the world in honoring the needs of families.

I'm an advocate for paid family and medical leave because the benefits are massive and forever. Unfortunately, we don't have the data on every good thing paid leave brings to families, but we can quantify some of the benefits. Paid parental leave is associated with fewer newborn and infant deaths, higher rates of breastfeeding, less postpartum depression, and a more active, hands-on role for new fathers. Mothers are much more likely to stay in the workforce and earn higher wages if they can take paid leave when they have a baby. And when men take leave, the redistribution of household labor and caretaking lasts after they return to work.

The lack of paid leave in the US is symptomatic of a workplace culture that also struggles with sexual harassment, gender bias, and a general indifference to family life. All these issues are aggravated by one reality: fewer women in positions of power. A male-dominated culture is more likely to emphasize paid leave's near-term costs and minimize its long-term benefits. There are huge personal benefits to workplaces that honor the obligations of family life, and those personal benefits turn into social and economic benefits as well. Unfortunately, those benefits aren't calculated when the low number of women in positions of power leaves the shaping of the culture to men who don't see and feel family needs as much as women do.

This is an immense challenge for us. It's especially hard for women to ask for money or power or promotions or even for more time with our families. It's easier to pretend we don't need these things. But workplace cultures that don't meet our needs persist when we're embarrassed by our needs. This has to change. If we're ever going to be who we are, we have to stand up collectively and ask for what we need in a culture that doesn't want us to have it. It's the only way to create a culture that meets the needs of everyone with a job.

We're quick to criticize gender injustice when we see it around the world. We also need to see it where most of us feel it and can do something about it—in the places where we work.

# CHAPTER NINE

# Let Your Heart Break

## *The Lift of Coming Together*

Earlier in the book, I told you I made a special trip to Sweden to have my last talk with Hans Rosling. In this final chapter, I want to tell you what he said.

It was 2016, and Hans was ill with cancer. He didn't have long to live, and he was working on a book that would be finished by his son and daughter-in-law after he died. I traveled to his home in southern Sweden, and Hans and his wife, Agneta, invited me to sit down and have breakfast with them in their kitchen. Hans and I knew it was the last time we'd see each other.

He had a lecture prepared for me, as he always did. It was a lecture he had given to me before—but if you're not repeating yourself by the end of your life, you haven't yet figured out what's true. Hans knew what was true, and he wanted to give me the lesson of his life one last time.

He pulled out a piece of paper, placed it on the table between our plates, and said, "Melinda, if you remember only one thing I've told you, remember that you have to go to the people on the margins." He took out a pen and sketched two roads running perpendicular and intersecting in the middle of the paper. Then he drew a river that ran through the point where the two roads met, and he said, "If you live near the crossroads or if you live near a river, you're going to be okay. But if you live on the margins"—and here he used his pen to mark the four corners of the page—"the world is going to forget about you."

"Melinda," he told me, "you can't let the world forget about them."

He was tearful when he told me this. It was the passion and obsession of his life, and he was asking me to carry it on.

The map Hans drew that day showed the geography of poverty. The extremely poor live far away from the flow of travel and trade that connects people to each other. But Hans would agree there is also a social geography of poverty. People might live in the middle of a large city but still be isolated from the flow of life. These people, too, live on the margins. I want to tell you about some women who live on the outermost margins—groups of sex workers in India who proved that when women organize, they can soar over every barrier described in this book. They can move the river and make it flow through them.

In 2001, when Jenn was 4 and Rory was 1, I took my first foundation trip to Asia. Rory was too young to ask questions, but Jenn wanted to know everything. "Mommy's going to be away for a week," I said. Then I stopped talking because I didn't know what to say to a 4-year-old about poverty and disease. After thinking for a moment, I told her about one part of the trip: I was going to visit children who didn't have homes and couldn't get medicine when they were sick. "What does that *mean*, they don't have homes?" she asked. I did my best to give her an answer that wouldn't be jarring, and then I went to my room to pack.

A few minutes later, she came running toward me carrying a bundle of blankets. "What's all this for?" I asked. "These are my special blankets," Jenn said. "I thought you could take them in case the kids don't have blankets." I thanked her profusely, and we both packed her blankets in my suitcase. Every time I called home from the trip, Jenn would ask, "Have you seen the kids yet? Do they like my blankets? Are you going to leave them there?"

I did leave them there, but I came back from that trip with more than I went with—especially more humility. I met a woman in Thailand who shook my world. She had a doctorate from Johns Hopkins and was a specialist in HIV epidemics. She spent several days touring villages with me, talking about what could be done to slow the spread of HIV. It was the number one global health emergency at the time, and health officials were predicting terrifying outbreaks, including tens of millions of new cases of HIV infection in India alone. I was a beginner in global health back then, just learning about the issues. Bill and I knew we had to take some action on AIDS, but we didn't know what. I was taking this trip to help us find out.

On my last day there, I was on a boat crossing a river near the borders with Laos and Burma, and my new friend said to me, "So now that you've been here a few days, if you were a woman and you were born here, what would you do to keep your children alive? What lengths would you go to?"

I was startled by the question, so I stalled for a minute and tried to put myself in that scene. *Okay, well, I would get a job. But I'm not educated. I can't even read. But I would teach myself to read. But with what books? And I'm not going to get a job because there are no jobs. I'm in a remote region.* I was trying to come up with an answer when she interrupted my thinking and said, "Do you know what I would do?" I said, "No. What would you do?" She answered, "Well, I've lived here for two years now. I know the options. I would be a sex worker. It would be the only way I could put food on the table."

It was a shocking thing to say. But after taking the whole trip in and reflecting for a while, it struck me that saying the opposite thing would have been even more shocking. If you say, "Oh, I would *never* do that," then you're saying you'd let your kids die—that you wouldn't do everything in your power to help them live. And you're saying something else, too. You're saying, "I'm above these people." She had worked with sex workers on other health crises, so her question to me had an edge to it, implied but still powerful: "How can you partner with them if you think you're above them?"

Two years after I returned from that trip, our foundation launched an HIV prevention program for India that relied on the leadership of sex workers. We called it Avahan, a Sanskrit word for "call to action." It was a high-stakes bet, not just because so many lives were at risk but because we didn't really know what we were doing. No one did. The world had never seen anything like this: a country with more than a billion people facing a deadly epidemic whose defeat would have to involve an extensive partnership with the most despised group in a deeply caste-conscious society. Ordinarily, we would launch a smaller program and build it up, but there wasn't time; we had to scale it up at the start. It became one of the largest HIV prevention projects in the world, with the goal of turning back the epidemic all across India.

Sex workers *had* to play a central role in the project because sex work was one of the critical pathways for the disease. If one person with HIV gave the infection to a sex worker, she could spread it to hundreds of customers, often truckers, who could in turn infect their wives, who might then pass the infection to their children during pregnancy, birth, or breastfeeding. If, however, sex workers were able to negotiate condom use with their clients, the sex workers' risk of becoming infected would plunge, and so would their risk of passing it on. That was the strategy—decrease the instances of unprotected sex between sex workers and their clients. But this ran into the challenge that can defeat even a great strategy: How can people be persuaded to drop one behavior and take up another? This is where Avahan turned into one of the most surprising and inspiring stories I've heard—and one of the most important lessons of my life.

In January of 2004, when Avahan was less than a year old, I made my second trip to India. It was a trip with my closest women friends, members of my spirituality group. We wanted to visit places for prayer and meditation and see religious sites, and we also wanted to learn about the services available to the poor and play a brief role in that if we could.

When we were there, staying in Calcutta, we got up in the morning before the sun rose and walked across the city to the Missionaries of Charity's motherhouse, where Mother Teresa started her work. At the motherhouse, there is a chapel where the nuns meet for prayer every morning, so we decided, though we're not all Catholics, that we would go to the chapel for Mass. On the way there, we had to step over homeless people sleeping on the sidewalk. It was morally wrenching. These are people that Mother Teresa would have stopped to help.

In the chapel, we met people from all over the world who came to volunteer for the day in one of Mother's homes. After Mass, we walked to the orphanage, where we were given a tour. My friends then stayed there to help the staff, and I left to meet with a group of sex workers to talk about HIV prevention.

At least I *thought* that's what we were going to talk about. The women I met wanted to talk to me about stigma, about how hard their lives were. And they wanted to talk about their children. I had a conversation with a woman named Gita who told me that her son, then in ninth grade, was on track for college. And she clenched her fists for emphasis when she told me that her daughter was doing well in school and was not going to become a sex worker. Gita and so many other women in the group made it clear that they were in sex work to provide for their families. They couldn't find another way, but they were determined that their daughters wouldn't be forced into the same choice.

Beyond our conversations, what struck me most about Gita and the other women I met was how much they wanted to touch and be touched. Nobody in the community touches a sex worker except to have sex with her. No matter what caste they're from, sex workers are untouchable. For them, touching is acceptance. So when we hugged, they held on. I've seen this again and again when I've met with sex workers of all genders. We talk and take a photo and hug— and they won't let go. If I turn to greet someone else, they hold on to my shirt or keep a hand on my shoulder. In the beginning I found it awkward. After a while, though, I melted into it. If they want to embrace a bit longer, I'm all in.

So I gave lots of hugs, and I listened to stories—harsh tales of rape and abuse, and hopeful stories about children. As our time together came to an end, the women said they wanted a group photograph, so we linked our arms and took a picture (which would appear in the next day's paper). I found that moment very emotional, and I was already on the edge. Then a few of the women started singing the civil rights anthem "We Shall Overcome" in Bengali-accented English, and I started to cry. I tried to hide it because I didn't know how they would interpret my tears. For me, the contrast between their determination and their dire circumstances was both inspiring and heartbreaking.

These women were our partners. They were the frontline defenders against AIDS in India, and we still didn't fully understand how brutal their lives were. They faced constant violence from their lovers, from their clients, who were themselves poor and marginalized, and from the police, who would harass them, arrest them, rob them, and rape them.

The brutality of their lives was a revelation even to our staff in India. In one case, members of our team met with four or five sex workers to have tea and conversation in a restaurant. Later that day, the sex workers were arrested because they had gathered together in a public place.

Shortly after that, one Avahan worker drove out to a coastal road near the Bay of Bengal where the truckers stop, so he could learn about the lives of sex workers there. He met with a group of women for a few hours—sitting on a mat, drinking tea, and asking about the program, what helped, what more was needed. When the meeting was over and people were saying their goodbyes, one of the sex workers started crying. Our team member was afraid he'd said something insensitive, so he asked one of the other women, "Did I do something wrong?" She said, "No, it's nothing." When he pleaded for an answer, the woman said, "She was crying because you, a respectable man, had come to meet her and talk to her politely as opposed to paying her for sex, and she thought it was such an honor that someone would come just to have tea with her."

Another story came from a partner of ours, a woman who was very devoted to improving the lives of sex workers in her area. She told us she was once at the bedside of a sex worker who was dying of AIDS, and the sex worker said, "Would you please fulfill my last wish?" "I'll do whatever I can," the woman replied. So the sex worker asked, "Can I call you Aai?" *Aai* in Marathi means "mother." That was her only wish, to call this loving woman there at her deathbed "mother." That's how hard their lives are.

## How Empowerment Starts

We hadn't taken the realities of sex workers' lives into account when we designed the Avahan program. We didn't think we had to. We wanted sex workers to insist on condom use with their clients, get treated for STDs, and get tested for HIV—and we thought it was enough to tell them about the benefits and ask them to do it. But it wasn't working, and we couldn't understand why. We had never imagined that something might be more important to them than preventing HIV.

"We don't need your help with condoms," they said, almost laughing. "We'll teach *you* about condoms. We need help preventing violence."

"But that's not what we do," our people said. And the sex workers answered, "Well, then you don't have anything interesting to tell us, because that's what we need."

So our team held debates about what to do. Some said, "Either we rethink our approach or we shut this down." Others said, "No, this is mission creep—we have no expertise in this area, and we shouldn't get involved."

Eventually, our team met again with the sex workers and listened intently as they talked about their lives, and the sex workers emphasized two things: One, preventing violence is their first and most urgent concern; two, fear of violence keeps them from using condoms.

Clients would beat up the women if they insisted on condoms. The police would beat them up if they were *carrying* condoms— because it proved they were sex workers. So to avoid getting beaten up, they wouldn't carry condoms. Finally we saw the connection between preventing violence and preventing HIV. The sex workers couldn't address the long-term threat of dying from AIDS unless they could address the near-term threat of being beaten, robbed, and raped.

So instead of saying, "It's beyond our mandate," we said, "We want to help protect you from violence. How can we do that?"

They said, "Today or tomorrow, one of us is going to get raped or beaten up by the police. It happens all the time. If we can get a dozen women to come running whenever this happens, the police will stop doing it." So our team and the sex workers set up a system. If a woman is attacked by the police, she dials a three-digit code, the code rings on a central phone, and twelve to fifteen women come to the police station yelling and shouting. And they come with a pro bono lawyer and a media person. If a dozen women show up shouting, "We want her out now or there's going to be a story in the news tomorrow!" the police will back down. They will say, "We didn't know. We're sorry."

That was the plan, and that's what the sex workers did. They set up a speed-dial network, and when it was triggered, the women came running. It worked brilliantly. One sex worker reported that she had been beaten up and raped in a police station a year before. After the new system was in place, she went back to the same police station and the policeman offered her a chair and a cup of tea. Once word of this program got out, sex workers in the next town came and said, "We want to join that violence prevention program, not the HIV thing," and soon the program spread all over India.

Why was this approach so effective? Ashok Alexander, then

head of our India office, put it bluntly, "Every man who's a bully is scared of a group of women."

We thought we were running an HIV prevention program, but we had stumbled onto something more effective and pervasive—the power of women coming together, finding their voices, and speaking up for their rights. We had begun funding women's empowerment.

Empowerment starts with getting together—and it doesn't matter how humble the gathering place is. The scene of empowerment for Avahan was community centers—often just small, one-room structures built of cinder blocks where the women could meet and talk. Remember, these women had no place to gather. If they met in public, the police would round them up and put them in jail. So when our team redesigned the program around violence prevention, they began to rent space and encourage the women to come and talk. The community centers became the place they could get services. They could get condoms. They could meet each other. They could take a nap. They weren't allowed to stay overnight, but in daytime hours, many of them would lie on the floor and sleep as their kids ran around. In some places, the team put in a beauty parlor or a space for playing board games. The centers became the place where things happened. And the idea came from the women themselves.

The opening of the first drop-in center was "the most beautiful thing I've ever seen," according to an early Avahan team member. Five women walked in, afraid they were going to be drugged and have their kidneys harvested. That was the rumor. Instead they were welcomed and told, "Just talk to each other. Drink three cups of chai and then leave." That's how empowerment began at Avahan—people on the outermost margins of society, excluded by everyone, coming together to talk, drink tea, and lift each other up.

Bill and I knew about the program's shift to violence prevention, but we were in the dark about the community centers, and this still makes me laugh. Ashok would come meet with us in Seattle and give us reports, but we didn't get the full story until Bill and I went to India together in 2005. Ashok was briefing us, explaining what we were about to see, and he started talking about these community centers, tiny spaces where sex workers could gather and talk. I remember saying to Bill after the briefing, "Did you know we were funding community centers?" He said, "No, did *you* know we were funding community centers?"

We had given Ashok the money, and he's a smart businessperson, so he set a strategy and tacked against it. He did everything he said he was going to do, and some things he never mentioned. And thank goodness for that, because the honest and embarrassing truth is that if he had come and presented the idea of community centers to us at the foundation, I think we would have said no. We would have seen it as too remote from our mission, which was to work on innovations and depend on others to get them out. Helping distribute condoms was already a big step away from our self-image as innovators who counted on others for delivery, but to work on violence prevention through empowerment nurtured in community centers—*that* would have been too radical for us, at least until we saw their value on that trip to India.

On that visit, Bill and I met with a group of sex workers. There is a photo of that event hanging prominently at the foundation office—Bill and I sitting cross-legged on the ground taking our place in the circle. At the start of our meeting, I asked one of the women, "Please tell us your story." She told us about her life. Then another woman told us how she got involved in sex work. Then a third woman shared a story that brought silence to the room, broken only by the sounds of sobbing. She told us she was a mom, she had a daughter, the father was not in the picture, and she had turned to sex work because she had no other options for income. She was making every sacrifice to create a better life for her daughter, who had lots of friends and was doing well in school. The mother had constantly worried, though, that as her daughter got older, she might find out how her mom made money. One day, exactly as the mother feared, her daughter's classmate announced to everyone at school that the girl's mother was a sex worker, and her friends began mocking her viciously and continuously in the cruelest ways. A few days later, the mother came home and found her daughter dead, hanging from a rope.

I shot a look at Bill. He was in tears. So was I, and so was everyone else in the room—especially the women whose wounds were opened up by this story. These women were in agony, but they were also full of empathy, and that eased their isolation. By coming together and sharing their stories, they gained a sense of belonging, and the sense of belonging gave them a feeling of self-worth, and the feeling of self-worth gave them the courage to band together and demand their rights. They were no longer outsiders; they were insiders. They had a family and a home. And slowly they began to dispel the illusion that society imposes on the disempowered: that because they are denied their rights, they have no rights; that because no one listens to them, they are not speaking the truth.

Brené Brown says that the original definition of courage is to let ourselves be seen. And I think one of the purest ways to let ourselves be seen is to ask for what we want—*especially* when no one wants us to have it. I just fall silent before that kind of courage. These women found that courage with the help of each other.

The impact of Avahan grew way beyond the accomplishments of that first group of women, and the story was not just about how inclusion and community empowered a group of outcasts. It was about what those outcasts did for their country. I'll give you two examples.

First, many years ago, about the same time that Bill and I made this trip to India, we were exploring different approaches to fighting AIDS, and we got super excited about a new possibility—that the drugs effective in treating AIDS could also work in *preventing* AIDS. We helped fund drug trials to test the idea, and the trials came back with spectacular findings: Oral prevention drugs can cut the risk of getting HIV through sex by more than 90 percent. The AIDS community's highest hopes were fulfilled. Then they were dashed.

The approach required healthy people to take pills every day, and the at-risk groups just didn't do it. Getting people to take up any new health behavior, no matter how effective, is frustratingly difficult. People have to be engaged, informed, and highly motivated. Tragically, AIDS activists and funders and governments and health workers just could *not* get people to take the drugs. Only two groups, worldwide, were an exception: gay white men in the United States . . . *and women sex workers in India.*

A study showed that 94 percent of Indian sex workers took the drugs faithfully and continuously. That level of compliance is unheard of in global health—and the study attributes it to the strong networks created by the women in Avahan.

That's the first example. Here's the second. In 2011, the British medical journal *The Lancet* published an article showing that the intensity of the Avahan work correlated with lower HIV prevalence in a number of India's most populous states. In the years since, it's been well documented that sex workers' insistence on condom use with their clients kept the epidemic from breaking more widely into the population. These empowered women became indispensable partners in a national plan that saved millions of lives.

In a country where no one would touch them, these women touched each other, and in that small society of acceptance, they began to discover and recover their dignity, and from their dignity came the will to demand their rights, and in asserting their rights, they were able to protect their lives and save their country from catastrophe.

## Finding Our Voices

More than ten years after Avahan led me on a path of women's empowerment, I was in New York City moderating a panel on women's social movements. One of my guests was the amazing Leymah Gbowee, who shared the 2011 Nobel Peace Prize with Ellen Johnson Sirleaf and Tawakkol Karman. Leymah was recognized, along with Ellen, for launching a women's peace movement that helped bring an end to the Liberian civil war.

Sometimes when I'm in the middle of the work—even when I think I know what I'm doing—I find that I really don't have a deep understanding of the forces at play until after the action is over. Then, sometimes years later, I look back and say, "Oh!! I get it." That's what Leymah offered me that day—not just an understanding of her peace movement, but how its principles helped explain the success of Avahan and so much more.

Leymah told us that she was living in her country as a 17-year-old when the first of two civil wars broke out there. After the end of the first war and before the start of the second, she studied peace activism and trauma healing and came to believe that "if any changes were to be made in society, it had to be by the mothers."

She was invited to Ghana to attend the first-ever meeting of the Women in Peacebuilding Network, which included women from nearly every West African nation. Leymah was named coordinator of the Liberian Women's initiative, and after the second civil war broke out, she began working around the clock for peace. One night, after again falling asleep in her office, she awoke from a dream where she'd been told, "Gather the women and pray for peace."

She went to the mosques on Friday, the markets on Saturday, and the churches on Sunday to recruit women for peace. She gathered thousands of Muslim and Christian women, led demonstrations and sit-ins, defied orders to disperse, and eventually was invited to make the case for peace to Liberian president Charles Taylor, with thousands of women demonstrating outside the presidential mansion. She won a grudging promise from Taylor to hold peace talks with the rebels in Accra, Ghana.

To keep up the pressure, Leymah and thousands of other women went to Accra and demonstrated outside the hotel that was hosting the talks. When progress stalled, Leymah led dozens of women inside the hotel, and more women kept coming until there were two hundred. They all sat down in front of the entrance to the meeting hall and sent a message to the mediator that the men would not be allowed to leave until they had a peace agreement.

The mediator, former Nigerian president Abdusalami Abubakar, gave his support to the women and allowed them to maintain their presence and their pressure right outside the hall. The activists were given credit for changing the atmosphere of the peace talks from "circuslike to somber," and within weeks, the parties had an agreement and the war was officially over.

Two years later, Ellen Johnson Sirleaf was elected president of Liberia, becoming the first woman elected head of state in Africa.

Many years later, when Leymah sat down with me in New York, I asked her why her movement was so effective. She said, "We women in these communities are the nurturers of society. And it was upon us to change it."

By 2003, she said, Liberia "had gone through over fourteen warring factions and made more than thirteen peace agreements. We said to ourselves, 'The men have done the same thing over and over. We have to bring some sense to the process. Instead of starting a women's warring faction, let's start a women's peace movement.'"

Then she told us an astonishing story about what that meant.

"There was one Muslim woman who had lost her daughter in the war," Leymah said. "She was part of our movement. She was feeding a fighter who had multiple gunshot wounds when he recognized her and said, 'Sit me up.' So she sat him up and he asked her, 'Where's your daughter?' She said, 'Oh, she died.' The fighter said, 'I know.' She said, 'How did you know?' He said, 'Because I killed her.'

"When she came back to the office, crying, we asked her, 'Did you stop feeding him?' and she said, 'No. Isn't that what peace means? Besides, I knew at that moment that I could come back to my sisters and we could cry together.'"

How did the women's movement succeed in bringing peace while the men's warring factions could not? Leymah's story says it all. When the women were wounded, they were able to absorb their pain without passing it on. But when the men were wounded, they needed to make someone pay. That's what fed the cycle of war.

I am *not* saying that women alone have the power of peacemaking and men alone are the cause of war. *Absolutely not*. I am saying that, *in this case*, the women were able to absorb their pain without passing it on and the men were not—*until they were prevailed upon by the women*! When the women found their voice, the men found their power to make peace. Each found the traditional attributes of the other inside themselves. The men were able to do something the women had done—agree not to retaliate—and the women were able to do something the men had done, which is to assert their views about how society should be run. Bringing these two qualities together is what brought peace.

Many successful social movements are driven by the same combination—strong activism and the ability to take pain without passing it on. Anyone who can combine those two finds a voice with moral force.

Leymah's friend who came back to cry with her sisters, and all the women who ever accepted their pain without passing it on, were not just sharing their grief but finding their voice—because their voice is buried underneath their grief. If we can face our pain, we can find our voice. And it is so much easier to face our pain and find our voice together.

When women are trapped in abuse and isolated from other women, we can't be a force against violence because we have no voice. But when women gather with one another, include one another, tell our stories to one another, share our grief with one another, *we find our voice with one another.* We create a new culture—not one that was imposed on us, but one we build with our own voices and values.

The first time I suspected a link between feeling our grief and finding our voice, I thought, *No way. If you need to feel your grief to find your voice, then why do people who can't take pain without passing it on have such loud voices?* Then it dawned on me: There is a big difference between a loud voice and a strong voice. The loud voice of a man who has no inner life and is a stranger to his own grief is never a voice for justice; it's a voice for self-interest, dominance, or vengeance. Strong male voices for freedom and dignity come from men like Gandhi, King, and Mandela who mastered their pain, gave up on vengeance, and preached forgiveness.

Nelson Mandela was once asked if he was still angry at his captors after he was released from prison, and he answered yes, he was still angry for a time, but he realized that if he stayed angry, he would still be a prisoner—and he wanted to be free.

When I think of the men who abuse women and girls, I don't

want to forgive them. It feels like that would be letting them get away with it. And I don't want to let them get away with anything. I fully support taking all possible steps to protect the innocent, including capturing perpetrators and meting out justice. But justice does not mean vengeance.

Desmond Tutu, who as chairman of the Truth and Reconciliation Commission kept South Africa from exploding in vengeance in the post-apartheid era, offers this path around revenge: "When I am hurt, when I am in pain, when I am angry with someone for what they have done to me, I know the only way to end these feelings is to accept them."

Dorothy Day, the Catholic social activist who used nonviolent action to serve the poor and homeless, said the greatest challenge is "how to bring about a revolution of the heart." The lesson I've learned from women in social movements all over the world is that to bring about a revolution of the heart, you have to let your heart break. Letting your heart break means sinking into the pain that's underneath the anger. This is how I make sense of the scriptural instruction "Resist not evil." I don't take this to mean "Make way for evil in the world." I think it means "Don't resist the feeling; accept the suffering." If you don't accept the suffering, hurt can turn to hatred. This is what the life of Christ means to me. The high priests wanted to break him. They did everything they could to hurt him and humiliate him. And they failed. His ability to absorb pain was beyond their ability to inflict it, so he could answer their hatred with love.

This, to me, is the model for all nonviolent social movements, religious based or not. The most radical approach to resistance is acceptance—and acceptance does *not* mean accepting the world as it is. It means accepting our *pain* as it is. If we refuse to accept our pain, then we're just trying to make ourselves feel better—and when our hidden motive is to make ourselves feel better, there is no limit to the damage we can do in the name of justice. Great leaders never combine a call for justice with a cry for vengeance. Leaders who can master their pain have taken self-interest off their agenda, so their voice rings with moral power. They are no longer speaking *their* truth. They are speaking truth.

The power of letting your heart break is not just something to admire in others. All of us have to let our hearts break; it's the price of being present to someone who is suffering. More than a decade ago, I was in South Africa with a highly respected medical doctor from the US. We went to a township near Johannesburg to visit the home of a man who was dying of AIDS. Our host was clearly tired and in pain, but he was graciously telling us his story when the doctor stood up and left. He made excuses, but I knew why he left, and I'm afraid the dying man did, too. The doctor, who had mostly focused on research, couldn't bear to see the tragic reality of this man's life. And if you can't bear the pain of your neighbor's suffering, then in one way or another, you're going to push that person to the margins.

Every society says its outsiders are the problem. But the outsiders are not the problem; the urge to create outsiders is the problem. Overcoming that urge is our greatest challenge *and* our greatest promise. It will take courage and insight, because the people we push to the margins are the ones who trigger in us the feelings we're afraid of.

Isolating others to ease our fears is a deep urge inside all of us. How do we turn it around?

## We Are One

If there is a point of unity across humanity, it's that all of us have been outsiders at some time in our lives—even if only as kids on the playground. And none of us liked it. We tasted it just enough to be terrified by it. In spite of that experience, though, many of us don't have any idea what it feels like to be wholly excluded.

That's why I was so taken by a passage in my mom's favorite book, *Life of the Beloved*, by Henri Nouwen. Nouwen was a Catholic priest with the mind of a genius and the heart of a saint. He taught at Notre Dame, Harvard, and Yale but lived the last years of his life in a home for people with disabilities, where his ministry included helping a severely disabled member with his morning routine.

In *Life of the Beloved*, Nouwen writes: "In my own community, with many severely handicapped men and women, the greatest source of suffering is not the handicap itself, but the accompanying feelings of being useless, worthless, unappreciated, and unloved. It is much easier to accept the inability to speak, walk, or feed oneself than it is to accept the inability to be of special value to another person. We human beings can suffer immense deprivations with great steadfastness, but when we sense that we no longer have anything to offer to anyone, we quickly lose our grip on life."

We all want to have something to offer. This is how we belong. It's how we feel included. So if we want to include everyone, then we have to help everyone develop their talents and use their gifts for the good of the community. That's what inclusion means—everyone is a contributor. And if they need help to become a contributor, then we should help them, because they are full members in a community that supports everyone.

## When Women Come Together

Every issue in this book is a door women must walk through, or a wall we must break through, to become full contributors—the right to decide whether and when to have children, to marry or not marry, to seek opportunity, attend a university, control our income, manage our time, pursue our goals, and advance in the workplace—*any* workplace. For the sake of women trapped in poverty and for women at every level of society who are excluded or intimidated by powerful men, women need to meet, talk, organize, and lead—so we can break down the walls and open the doors for everyone.

I've been involved in women's groups my whole life, though sometimes I didn't recognize it until later. My all-girls high school was one large women's group. In college and graduate school, I sought out the women I admired, especially when there were few of us. As an adult, I nurtured connections with women in every realm of life—professional, personal, spiritual. I have always had many important male friends, and they've been indispensable to my happiness. But it's my women friends I come back to, especially in groups, when I'm facing my fears and need friends to help me through; they've walked beside me on every path of growth I took. I believe women's groups are essential for each of us individually but also for society generally—because progress depends on inclusion, and inclusion begins with women.

I'm not saying we should include women and girls *as opposed to* men and boys, but *along with them and on behalf of them*. This is not about bringing women in and leaving others out. It's about bringing women in as a way to bring *everyone* in.

Women must leave the margins and take our place—not above men or below them, but beside them—at the center of society, adding our voices and making the decisions we are qualified and entitled to make.

There will be plenty of resistance, but lasting progress will not come from a power struggle; it will come from a moral appeal. As we bring gender bias out from behind its disguises, more and more men and women will see bias where they hadn't suspected it and will stand against it. That's how we change the norms that hide the biases we were blind to. We *see* them, and we end them.

It's not easy to transform a culture built on exclusion. It's hard to cooperate with people who want to dominate. But we don't have a choice. We can't just make the insiders into the new outsiders and call it change. We have to include everyone, even those who want to exclude us. It's the only way to build the world we want to live in. Others have used their power to push people out. We have to use our power to bring people in. We can't just add one more warring faction. We have to end factions. It's the only way we become whole.

# Epilogue

I've been saying from the beginning of this book that equality can empower women, and empowered women will change the world. But in the end (and we are at the end), I have to confess that, for me, equality is a milestone; it is not the summit.

The supreme goal for humanity is not equality but connection. People can be equal but still be isolated—not feeling the bonds that tie them together. Equality without connection misses the whole point. When people are connected, they feel woven into each other. You are part of me and I am part of you. I can't be happy if you're sad. I can't win if you lose. If either of us suffers, we suffer together. This blurs the borders between human beings, and what flows through those porous borders is love.

Love is what makes us one.

It ends the urge to push the other out. That is the goal. The goal is not for everyone to be equal. The goal is for everyone to be connected. The goal is for everyone to belong. The goal is for everyone to be loved.

Love is what lifts us up.

When we come together, we rise. And in the world we're building together, everyone rises. No one is exploited because they're poor or excluded because they're weak. There is no stigma and no shame and no mark of inferiority because you're sick, or because you're old, or because you're not the "right" race, or because you're the "wrong" religion, or because you're a girl or a woman. There is no wrong race or religion or gender. We have shed our false boundaries. We can love without limits. We see ourselves in others. We see ourselves *as* others.

That is the moment of lift.

If I ever see myself as separate or superior, if I try to lift myself up by pulling others down, if I believe people are on a journey I have completed, doing personal work I have mastered, attempting tasks I've accomplished—if I have any feeling that I am above them instead of trying to rise with them, then I have isolated myself from them. And I have cut myself off from the moment of lift.

I told you earlier about Anna, the woman whose family Jenn and I stayed with in Tanzania. She made such an emotional impression on me that I have her picture up on the wall in my home where I see it every day. I told you much of what bonded me to Anna, but I held something back so I could tell it to you now.

As I trailed her through her day of chores, trying to be a help or at least not a hindrance, Anna and I were talking about our lives, and then she opened up, as women often do, and told me of a crisis in her marriage.

When Anna and Sanare got married, Anna moved from her part of the country to Sanare's region, which was drier and demanded more work to farm and find water. Anna's walk to the well was twelve miles—each way. She adjusted to the extra work, but after the birth of their first child, she just couldn't bear it anymore. She packed her bags, gathered their child, and sat on their doorstep waiting. When Sanare returned from the fields, he found Anna ready to leave. She told him she was going back to her father's house to live because life was too hard in his homeland. Sanare was heartbroken and asked what he could do to make her stay. "Go fetch the water," Anna said, "so I can nurse our son." So Sanare broke Maasai tradition and walked to the well to get water. Later, he bought a bicycle and biked the distance to the well. The other men mocked him for doing women's work. They said he was bewitched by his wife. But Sanare was tough. He didn't budge. He knew his new chore would make his son healthier and make his wife happier, and that was enough for him.

After a time, some of the other men decided to join Sanare, and when they soon got tired of biking twenty-four miles to fetch water, they brought the community together to build catchment areas to collect rainwater near the village. As I listened to Anna's story, my heart filled with love for the courage it took for her to stand up to the traditions of her society, and for Sanare to do the same. She took a stand she knew would either destroy her marriage or deepen it, and I felt an inexpressible bond with her. We were in communion, holding our own impromptu women's group for two. And it occurred to me in a moment of private embarrassment that the rich American lady who was here to help had some gender equity issues of her own she needed to face, had a culture of her own she needed to change. This was not me helping Anna; it was me listening to Anna, and Anna inspiring me. It was two women from different worlds, meeting on the margins, and summoning a moment of lift.

# Acknowledgments

When I first began working on this book, I knew I wanted to share the stories of the women I've met and what I've learned from them. I didn't realize how much more I would learn and grow from the process of writing the book. My debt and gratitude are boundless.

Charlotte Guyman, Mary Lehman, Emmy Neilson, and Killian Noe, you define friendship for me. Thank you for encouraging me to write this book, for reading and commenting on drafts, and for teaching me the power of women's support and friendship.

To the women in my spiritual group, thank you for nurturing my spirituality and helping me deepen my faith. My debt to you all is infinite.

To my many teachers around the world, especially the women (and men) who welcomed me into their homes and communities, told me of their dreams, and taught me about their lives—thank you from the bottom of my heart. I'm grateful above all to Anna and Sanare, Chrissy and Gawanani, and *their* children who not only invited me and *my* children into their homes, but let us stay several nights. No visits have ever taught me more.

There are a number of women and men I've been lucky enough to meet in my life who have taught me truths that will last a lifetime—my teachers at Ursuline Academy, especially Susan Bauer and Monica Cochran; my teachers in faith and action, especially Fr. Richard Rohr and Sister Sudha Varghese; and my mentors and role models in creating change in the world, especially Hans Rosling, Bill Foege, Jimmy and Rosalynn Carter, Paul Farmer, Molly Melching, Patty Stonesifer, and Tom Tierney. There is no end to what I owe them.

There is no chance I would ever have been able to do any of this work without the amazing support of caregivers who over the years did more for my family than I can say, helping care for my children and ease my worries when I was at the foundation, on the road and away from home. There is no way to fully express my gratitude.

Sue Desmond-Hellmann, Mark Suzman, Josh Lozman, Gary Darmstadt, and Larry Cohen have been remarkable colleagues in so many ways. I'm grateful for all they've done and thank them for reading drafts of the book and offering their insights.

I want to thank Leslie Koch for shepherding this project from its inception; George Gavrilis and Ellie Schaack for their research and assistance; and Julie Tate for fact-checking the manuscript.

My irreplaceable friend and colleague John Sage convinced me that writing this book was a good idea, that I *could* find the time, and that others might want to hear the lessons I've learned from the women and men I've met in my work. My gratitude for John's vision and advice is endless.

Warren Buffett has been a generous friend in every imaginable way, believing so strongly in women and offering constant encouragement to me as I made the decision to become a public advocate. He is the mentor of a lifetime, and I can never thank him enough.

I'm indebted to my entire team at Pivotal Ventures, especially Haven Ley, Ray Maas, Catherine St-Laurent, Amy Rainey, Courtney Wade, and Windy Wilkins for reading the book and helping me improve it—and Clare Krupin, who traveled with me to so many places and helped me capture the stories of the women we met.

Paola Quinones, Megan Marx, Michele Boyer, Abby Page, Amy Johnston, and Melissa Castro offered flawless assistance on logistics, as did Carol Stults, Joseph Janowiak, Kelly Gilbert, and Sheila Allen.

The entire team at Flatiron was incredibly enthusiastic and supportive throughout—in particular Bob Miller, Amy Einhorn, Nancy Trypuc, Marlena Bittner, Amelia Possanza, Cristina Gilbert, Keith Hayes, Alan Bradshaw, and also Whitney Frick.

My editor at Flatiron, the incomparable Will Schwalbe, was a highlight of the whole experience for me. Will gave me not only guidance, but wisdom—sharing the knowledge of a lifetime in short truths that helped me navigate hard moments. His insights and his edits made the work a joy.

I am beyond grateful to Tom Rosshirt. I could not have written this book without him. Tom challenged me throughout to focus on what I wanted to accomplish and helped me in myriad ways. He's a brilliant writing partner and a deeply intuitive friend.

Finally, I want to thank my family, who not only encouraged me in writing the book, but inspired the love and values that started me in this work in the first place. My parents, who gave me a childhood steeped in the deep values of faith and love; my sister, Susan, and my brothers Raymond and Steven, who share everything with me, especially love and laughter; my children, Jenn, Rory, and Phoebe, who constantly inspire me to grow; and my husband and life partner, Bill. The most important lessons of my life are those I learned alongside you. Your faith in my growth, your eagerness to learn, and your optimism for the world and our work together are among the great sustaining forces of my life. My gratitude for your partnership through all of the adventures of life is inexpressible.

# Resource Guide of Organizations That Readers Can Support

I've listed below some of the organizations you've read about in this book. If their programs inspire you, you can visit their websites and learn how you can use your voice to advance their work.

### Bangladesh Rural Advancement Committee

*www.brac.net*

BRAC's mission is to empower people and communities in situations of poverty, illiteracy, disease, and social injustice.

### CARE

*www.care.org/our-work*

Women are a vital part of CARE's community-based efforts to improve basic education, increase access to quality healthcare, and expand economic opportunity for all.

## Family Planning 2020

*www.familyplanning2020.org*

FP2020 is working with governments, civil society, multilateral organizations, donors, the private sector, and the research and development community to enable 120 million more women and girls to use contraceptives by 2020.

## Girls Not Brides

*www.girlsnotbrides.org*

Girls Not Brides is a global partnership of more than 1,000 civil society organizations from over 95 countries committed to ending child marriage and enabling girls to fulfill their potential.

## Kakenya's Dream

*www.kakenyasdream.org*

Kakenya's Dream leverages girls' education to empower girls and transform rural communities.

## Malala Fund

*www.malala.org*

Malala Fund is working for a world where every girl can learn and lead.

## #MeToo movement

*www.metoomvmt.org*

The "me too" movement supports survivors of sexual violence and their allies.

## Population Council

*www.popcouncil.org*

The Population Council conducts research and programs to address critical health and development issues in more than 50 countries.

## PRADAN

*www.pradan.net*

PRADAN works in the poorest regions of India to help vulnerable communities organize collectives that help people, especially women, earn a decent living and support their families.

## Saksham

*www.community.org.in/story*

The Community Empowerment Lab is a community-entrenched global health research and innovation organization based in Uttar Pradesh, India. It grew out of the Saksham project described in chapter 2.

## Save the Children

*www.savethechildren.org*

Save the Children works worldwide to inspire breakthroughs in the way the world treats children and to achieve immediate and lasting change in their lives.

## Tostan

*www.tostan.org*

Tostan is an Africa-based organization working directly with rural communities that are leading their own development.

* * *

*For more information about the Bill & Melinda Gates Foundation, please visit www.gatesfoundation.org.*

*To learn more about how we can all work together to lift up women around the world, please visit www.momentoflift.com.*

*Melinda will be donating all the amounts she receives from the sale of this book to the organizations listed in this resource guide.*

**Melinda Gates** is a philanthropist, businesswoman, and global advocate for women and girls. As the co-chair of the Bill & Melinda Gates Foundation, Melinda sets the direction and priorities of the world's largest philanthropy. She is also the founder of Pivotal Ventures, an investment and incubation company working to drive social progress for women and families in the United States. Melinda grew up in Dallas, Texas. She received a bachelor's degree in computer science from Duke University and an M.B.A. from Duke's Fuqua School. Melinda spent the first decade of her career developing multimedia products at Microsoft before leaving the company to focus on her family and philanthropic work. She lives in Seattle, Washington, with her husband, Bill. They have three children, Jenn, Rory, and Phoebe.

www.momentoflift.com